# FOREST MAGIC

# FOREST MAGIC

### Rituals and Spells for
## GREEN WITCHCRAFT

### NIKKI VAN DE CAR

### Illustrated by
### ELIN MANON

RUNNING PRESS
PHILADELPHIA

Running Press
Hachette Book Group
1290 Avenue of the Americas, New York, NY 10104
www.runningpress.com
@Running_Press

Printed in China

First Edition: March 2024

Published by Running Press, an imprint of Hachette Book Group, Inc.
The Running Press name and logo are trademarks of Hachette Book Group, Inc.

The Hachette Speakers Bureau provides a wide range of authors for speaking events.
To find out more, go to www.hachettespeakersbureau.com or email HachetteSpeakers@hbgusa.com.

Running Press books may be purchased in bulk for business, educational, or promotional use. For more information, please contact your local bookseller or the Hachette Book Group Special Markets Department at Special.Markets@hbgusa.com.

The publisher is not responsible for websites (or their content) that are not
owned by the publisher.

Print book cover and interior design by Susan Van Horn.

Library of Congress Cataloging-in-Publication Data
Names: Van De Car, Nikki, author. | Manon, Elin, illustrator.
Title: Forest magic : rituals and spells for green witchcraft / Nikki Van De Car ; illustrated by Elin Manon.
Description: First edition. | Philadelphia : Running Press, 2024. | Includes index.
Identifiers: LCCN 2023027405 | ISBN 9780762485338 (hardcover) | ISBN 9780762485345 (ebook)
Subjects: LCSH: Magic--Miscellanea. | Witchcraft--Miscellanea. | Plants--Religious aspects--Neopaganism. | Forests and forestry--Religious aspects--Paganism. | Incantations.
Classification: LCC BF1623.P5 V36 2024 | DDC 133.4/3--dc23/eng/20230725
LC record available at https://lccn.loc.gov/2023027405

ISBNs: 978-0-7624-8533-8 (hardcover), 978-0-7624-8534-5 (ebook)

APS

10  9  8  7  6  5  4  3  2  1

*to the witches of the forest*

# CONTENTS

**PART**

# THE OAK KING

PART

# THE HOLLY KING

# INTRODUCTION

## *Women of the Woods*

Call forth an image of a woman of the woods. She lives a solitary and self-sufficient life, secure in her own power, with the knowledge that she can trust the forest to provide for her. She steps softly, her feet pressing gently into the mossy floor, the ferns brushing her ankles in a gentle greeting as she passes. The creatures know her—the deer do not startle, the chipmunks skitter up the path before her, and the birds watch her from the branches above. She gathers only what she needs—

mushrooms, berries, leaves, and vines; branches, grasses, needles, and twigs—murmuring a blessing and a thank-you to each as she moves by. When she passes a tree that needs tending—whether from bark rubbed by a deer's antlers, tiny branches growing from the base of the trunk, or a vine that has twisted where it is unwelcome—she stops, mending the forest as it requires. Each breath she inhales is a gift from the woods and each breath she exhales is a gift she offers in return.

We cannot all be Baba Yaga or Circe or any of the other witches of the woods, and yet we are their legacy. It is our birthright to carry on their traditions, in whichever ways work best for us. We don't need to dwell alone on an island, much less in a house with chicken legs, to practice forest magic. We don't even need to live in a cottage in the woods. While forest magic may seem impossibly far away from an apartment in the city, the truth is that it is around us always wherever we are. There is no city on this earth that doesn't have *some* form of forest life—it is there in the weeds that grow through the cracks in the sidewalk, the trees that loom over park benches, the abandoned lots littered with cornflowers and Queen Anne's lace. The forest is where the *wild* dwells, and the wild dwells everywhere.

But it does need our help. There's a term called *rewilding*, which refers to conservation efforts to bring back and allow room for the wild places, returning them to their natural uncultivated state. Examples include the reintroduction of wolves to Yellowstone National Park and bison to Montana; the removal of dams to allow fish to make their annual pilgrimages; and even the creation of bridges for animals to facilitate migration across highways. Each of these efforts is substantive, scientific forest magic at work.

Our forests burn, recede, and disappear, and it is our sacred duty as witches of the woods to serve them in any way we can. We can—and must—protect them through political action, including letter-writing—

since a letter is a powerful spell sent out into the world—donating whatever and whenever we can, using our power as consumers wisely, and, of course, voting. But we can also take it upon ourselves to work our will in more tactile ways, particularly when systemic change—which is always a slow process—feels overwhelmingly difficult.

That's where this book comes in. *Forest Magic* will serve as your lodestar in tending to and harnessing the power of the woods. It will guide you toward finding and creating your own sacred grove—the part of the world's forest that you will take on as yours to tend—teaching you to care for it as it will care in turn for you. This book will teach you how to channel the power of the forest throughout the year, the seasons, and the day. As you move through the Wheel of the Year, you will pause at each pagan holiday, or sabbat, and discover the plants that resonate most with that time. You will study their magical properties and discover ways to work your own spells with them—though please note that they should not be consumed unless it's specifically stated that it's safe to do so. (Even so, always consult an expert or medical professional to be sure a particular plant friend is right for your body.)

For ease, the general guidelines in the chapters that follow assume a location in North America. If that doesn't describe you, don't worry—it doesn't describe me, either! Depending on where you live, the weather conditions, and the topography of the land, these plants may not grow near you at these times or at all. But there is still so much to learn about and from all of these plants and trees.

Forest magic is both a gift and a responsibility. Whatever we take from the forest, we must return in kind, creating a cycle of support, potential, and magic that will grow with each passing day. As this exchange of power continues to swell, it will create a sustainable, healing restoration for our forests—and therefore for us all. Let's rewild our forests . . . and ourselves.

# FINDING AND CREATING
# YOUR SACRED GROVE

Sacred groves are groups of trees that have particular importance. They can be found all over the world, including in Ireland and other Celtic regions, Germanic countries, Greece, Italy, India, Japan, Eastern Europe, North America, and West and South Africa. One of the most ancient sacred groves is in Greece—the oak grove at Dodona. In Celtic cultures, sacred groves were known as *nemeton*, after the goddess Nemetona, who was honored there. When Abraham planted a grove in Beersheba and spoke the Name of God, he was creating a sacred grove.

Sacred groves remained plentiful up until the first century BCE, when the Romans attacked the modern-day United Kingdom. But in spite of that, many remain, and apart from their spiritual significance, they play a powerful ecological role. The Buoyem sacred grove in Ghana protects more than 20,000 fruit bats, and the sacred forests in West Africa serve as ecological preservation sites, as well as carbon sinks that help offset the climate crisis. There are thousands of sacred groves in India—some estimate as many as 100,000—and they keep rare and endangered plants and animals safe.

Finding, choosing, and creating your own sacred grove may be as simple as stepping outside, as some witches' groves are right in their own backyards. For others, tending them may require a journey—sometimes brief and sometimes a bit longer.

Close your eyes and ask yourself, *Do I already know my sacred grove?*

It may be a location from your childhood or somewhere you've gone hiking or swimming. It may be a place you picnic or a group of trees you jog beneath or walk through on your lunch break. It may be just one tree rather than a group of them—which is part of a sacred tradition that includes the Buddha's bodhi tree, ancient camphor trees, and banyan trees.

If a variety of choices come to mind, jot them all down in a journal. Write down a memory for each and consider sketching or painting each forest. Once you know them well and are clear on them in your heart and your mind, choose between them.

If this choice feels challenging, that's okay! We are meant to have connections to several forests, and you will likely feel called to tend multiple sacred groves over the course of your lifetime. This choice is not forever or to the exclusion of any other place—it's more a question of, *Which forest do I feel called to tend right now, today?*

If you cannot think of a single one that feels right to you, that's okay, too. These things can take time to reveal themselves.

Start by taking a walk. You can simply stroll out your front door, heading for the nearest group of trees you can find, or you can venture farther away, seeking a place filled with nature that feels magical to you. Either way, walk around with open eyes and a seeking heart. Brush any branches you pass with your fingertips. Listen to the rustle of the leaves in the wind. If there are leaves on the ground, step on them, feeling and hearing their crunch. Take your time. The answers will come when you are ready, so this walk may be fifteen minutes long or may take a few hours. You may find your grove today, or you may happen upon it on another walk, on another day. Right now, you are simply exploring. As you journey, continually ask yourself the following questions:

*Do I feel called to sit beneath a tree?* Some trees feel welcoming, with a sense that others have sat beneath them, generation after generation. Others seem secret, as if the shelter they offer is meant only for a chosen few. And still others feel unwilling, as if they are too shy or simply not ready to accept company.

*Do I hear a song in the murmuring of the leaves?* It may be a song you know or something just outside your range of thought, like a sensation you can't quite grasp.

*Do I feel a reverence in my heart?* Sacred groves are, after all, sacred, and they should evoke reverence. That doesn't mean you can't laugh or play or shout within them. (Play is absolutely a way to respect and tend to your sacred grove.) But there should still be a slight sense of awe, of awareness that these entities have power.

**Do I feel known, recognized, or accepted here?** We don't just choose our sacred groves—they choose us, too. It is a decision made in tandem, and as you recognize your sacred grove, it should also know you. This is a place where you can be all that you are in full, where you can weep and rage and rejoice and reflect—the trees will accept it all.

If the answer to any or all of these questions is yes, you may have found your sacred grove.

It can be as simple as that! Magic doesn't require anything more than choice and intention. Sometimes, however, it can feel right to perform a ritual—sealing the deal, so to speak.

Choose a tree to sit beneath. Nestle yourself amongst its roots, aligning your spine with its trunk. If you can lean against the tree, do so, but if not, simply let *your* trunk, the vertical line of your body, match up with the tree's stretching energy. Close your eyes and listen to your tree, as well as all the others in your grove. Maybe they are all in a line, planted along a shaded city street. Maybe they are grouped in a park. Or maybe you've found a forest off a hiking trail. Maybe the trees are tall and majestic, or maybe they are young, newly planted, and fiercely energetic. Your grove is *yours*, and it is whatever you need, as well as whatever needs you.

Feel the tickle of grass or the press of rocks beneath you. Smell the loam of the earth and the cool, damp air of the forest. Listen to the creaking of the branches and the song of the leaves. Listen to the birds as they fly past and to any insects or creatures that make their home in or beneath the trees. You are one of them now. Visualize the network of branches stretching up and out and the mirrored network of roots stretching down and away, surrounding you, sheltering you from above and below.

Say aloud or in your mind, *I choose you. Do you choose me?*

Listen for the answer.

Visit your grove often. Get to know every single tree, checking over them and giving them your love. Slowly, you will come to learn the animals that live here by the signs they leave. Over the course of the year, you will watch how your sacred grove changes, sprouting new growth, sending its seeds forth into the world, settling in for a long wintry sleep. You can meditate within its shelter, ask it for advice, and share with it your joys and sorrows. You are its caretaker, watching over it, ministering to it, and protecting it for the generations that will come after you.

## ON ASKING PERMISSION

When practicing forest magic—or indeed any magic that involves another living thing—it is important to work with full consent and participation. This is particularly crucial when we're talking about harvesting herbs or taking cuttings from trees, because this is typically not beneficial for the plant. There are exceptions, of course, as pruning can promote growth and thinning can help herbs to grow, but in general these plants are giving us a piece of themselves, and we should request their permission to receive these blessings.

Asking permission can be as simple as a whispered "please," a respectful nod, or even a silent intention. But for something a little more involved, you might consider the following ritual.

First, choose an offering. This can be a smooth stone you've found nearby, a fallen leaf that caught your eye, or a libation poured from your water bottle. Kneel before the plant in question, and bow your head. Close your eyes, and allow yourself to come into alignment with the plant's rhythm. Every plant draws its own kind of breath, so use your imagination and intuition to find that same breath within yourself. Reach out with your nondominant hand and touch the plant, whether by brushing its leaves with your fingertips, stroking its petals, or pressing your palm against its bark.

If any words of gratitude come to you, speak them, either aloud or in your heart. When it feels right, take what you need—no more and no less. When you've finished, dig a small hole near the plant with your fingertips, and place or pour your offering there, setting your intentions for returning to the plant what was given to you threefold.

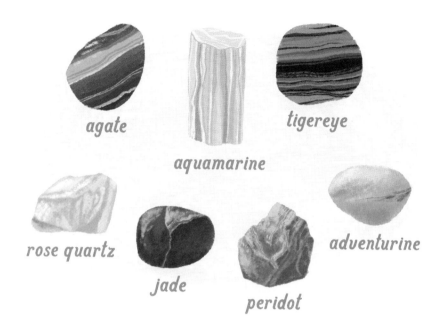

agate

aquamarine

tigereye

rose quartz

jade

peridot

adventurine

# CRYSTALS AND FOREST MAGIC

Crystals are a part of the natural world. They are formed when liquid elements like carbon, calcium, and silica harden and meld together to form a lattice—a repeating pattern—within their structural makeup.

Essentially, they're really pretty rocks. But they've been formed over the course of millions of years, growing with the same kind of slow ponderance as the pines, sequoias, junipers, and cypresses that live for thousands of years. And just like the trees in our forests, each crystal is different. Their internal geometric structures vary from type to type, and with that divergence comes a variety of different energies.

Just as the plants in this book have certain magical properties—gifts that we can receive with an open heart and mind—crystals also have magical and energetic gifts. Some of the spells here will recommend the use of certain crystals to support the natural attributes of the plants, so here is a quick primer on the suggested crystals and their meanings.

**AGATE** • Brings courage, strength, and confidence in your own abilities.

**AMETHYST** • Provides calm and tranquility in meditation, and can help you develop your intuition.

**AQUAMARINE** • Helps you express your innermost self.

**AVENTURINE** • Known as the "stone of opportunity," it will provide you with both luck and wealth.

**BLACK TOURMALINE** • A protective stone that places an energetic boundary around you, sealing out any negativity.

**BLUE LACE AGATE** • Will help you release anger so you can communicate clearly.

**CALCITE** • Amplifies your energy so you can better communicate with the unseen world.

**CARNELIAN** • Enhances creativity and sensuality.

**CHRYSOCOLLA** • Also known as the goddess stone, it will help you tap into your feminine power.

**FLUORITE** • Aids in concentration and decision-making.

**JADE** • Helps boost ambition, as well as longevity.

**LAPIS LAZULI** • This powerful stone of focus boosts your psychic ability.

**MOOKAITE** • Known as the "stone of adventure," mookaite will usher you onto your path with the knowledge that many forks lie ahead.

**OBSIDIAN** • Will protect you from forces you cannot see, and will help you not only face, but understand, that which you fear most.

**OPAL** • Will amplify your mystical powers and invite creativity.

**PERIDOT** • Symbolic of the sun, it will invite energy, positivity, and light.

**PYRITE** • Also known as "fool's gold," pyrite offers both protection and energy.

**ROSE QUARTZ** • A stone of sweet and gentle love.

**SMOKY QUARTZ** • Good for focus and fertility, as well as protection, as it kicks your survival instincts into high gear.

**SUNSTONE** • Invites a sense of happiness and well-being, and stimulates energy to move freely through the body.

**TIGEREYE** • Increases your own personal power and sense of integrity.

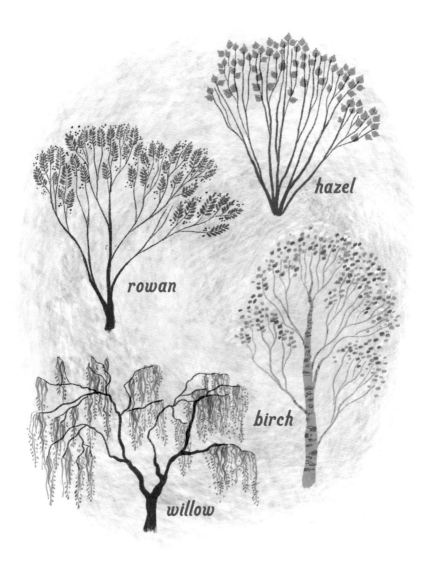

rowan

hazel

birch

willow

# THE CALENDAR OF THE TREES

Every culture in history formed some method of tracking the seasons—their own calendar—and they often did so using the night sky as a guide. The stars shift overhead, and the moon goes through her cycle. These mystical yet predictable constants have steered Native American, Hawaiian, Chinese, Arabic, Hebrew, Hindu, Māori cultures . . . and the list goes on and on. Even Western astrology, with its sun signs (Aries, Leo, Sagittarius, and so forth), is based on these same celestial coordinates. There is so much to explore in the skies.

For the purposes of forest magic, however, let's turn to a lesser known but quite relevant calendar: the Celtic tree calendar. There is some question as to how historical it actually is—there is some sparse evidence to suggest that it dates back to 8,000 BCE, while other research seems to indicate it was a pseudo-invention of the poet/historian Robert Graves in 1948. Graves based this calendar on the works of Roderick O'Flaherty, a historian in the late 1700s, and possibly also on the fourteenth-century *Book of Ballymote*, which contains a description of Ogham, the ancient Celtic alphabet of trees—which indisputably does have historical origins.

Regardless of when or how this calendar of trees came to be, it is a wonderful example of the ways in which magic, much like language, continues to evolve. We are constantly forming new ways of connecting with the mystical and spiritual powers of our world. And this is a *good* thing—it reminds us that, while we are as eternal as the faraway stars, we are also unfixed. We too can move and change, creating new pathways and possibilities . . . new magic in our own lives.

# Ogham

This early medieval Celtic alphabet can be found inscribed into stone pillars scattered across what is now Ireland, Scotland, and Wales. Some theories suggest that it was created as a form of covert communication—a way for people to leave secret messages for one another that couldn't be intercepted by the invading Roman Empire. These days, Ogham is often used for divination, much like Norse runes (Futhark) or the I Ching.

Each of the letters of the Ogham alphabet is named for a tree, and they are traditionally inscribed onto five sticks, with each stick growing upward and forming, in essence, a tree of trees.

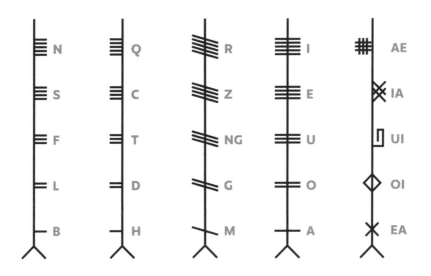

**B, BEITH** • The birch tree, representative of new beginnings, change, and purification

**L, LUIS** • The rowan tree, representative of insight, protection, and blessings

**F, FEARN** • The alder tree, representative of the connection between the seen and unseen worlds

**S, SAILLE** • The willow tree, representative of knowledge and spiritual growth

**N, NION** • The ash tree, representative of the connection between the inner and outer self and of creativity

**H, HUATH** • The hawthorn tree, representative of cleansing, protection, and defense

**D, DUIR** • The oak tree, representative of strength, resilience, and self-confidence

**T, TINNE** • The holly tree, representative of immortality, courage, and protection

**C, COLL** • The hazel tree, representative of life, wisdom, creativity, and knowledge

**Q, QUERT** • The apple tree, representative of love, faith, and rebirth

**M, MUIN** • The vine, representative of prophecy and truth

**G, GOT** • The ivy, representative of growth, wildness, and the cycle of rebirth

**NG, NGEATAL** • The reed, representative of health, healing, and community

**Z/ST, STRAITH** • The blackthorn tree, representative of authority, strength, and control

**R, RUIS** • The elder tree, representative of endings, maturity, and wisdom

**A, AILIM** • The elm tree, representative of flexibility, clarity of vision, and long-term goals

**O, ONN** • The gorse, representative of long-term plans, determination, and perseverance

**U, UHR** • The heather, representative of passion, generosity, and healing

**E, EADHADH** • The aspen, representative of endurance, courage, and success

**I, IODHADH** • The yew, representative of endings, rebirth, and change

**EA, EABHADH** • The grove, representative of multiple trees, symbolizing connection, conflict resolution, and justice

**OI, OUR** • The spindle tree, representative of strength, hard work, and family

**UI, UILLEAN** • The honeysuckle, representative of strong will, desires, and dreams

**IA, IFIN** • The pine, representative of clarity of vision and the release of guilt

**AE, AMHANCHOLL** • The witch hazel, representative of purity, cleansing, and new beginnings

# *The Zodiac of Trees*

The calendar of trees is based on lunar cycles, rather than the Gregorian calendar, so it tends to shift—but here is a basic guide to finding your tree sign. We will cover each of these trees in more detail throughout the book, but this section will get you started in understanding your tree-as-personality type.

⊢

## BIRCH

### *(December 24—January 20)*

Birch tends to be high-energy and ambitious. They are constantly striving and are tough enough to withstand whatever life might throw their way. They are a natural leader and can inspire others to reach great heights.

⊨

## ROWAN

### *(January 21—February 17)*

A naturally philosophical creature, Rowan is intuitive and idealistic. They bring a new perspective to any given situation, though they are often quiet and will keep their opinions to themselves unless pressed. That said, their inner fire burns bright, and their creativity has the potential to bring great change to the world.

☰

## ASH

### *(February 18—March 15)*

Ash is imaginative and artistic. Their vivid inner world can make them a little moody at times, but their sense of wonder and possibility—as well as their intuition and creativity—allows them to understand their own identity in a deep and ever-growing way.

 xxvii

## ALDER
### *(March 16—April 14)*

Alder is the Leo of the zodiac of the trees. They are passionate, fiery, and charismatic. They are confident and utterly themselves—which, of course, tends to draw others to them. Their confidence helps them to explore new possibilities.

## WILLOW
### *(April 15—May 12)*

Willow has a gentle nature and a sense that all things, good and bad, will pass—the cycle will always continue. Their emotional as well as intellectual intelligence makes them successful in their career and relationships. They have extraordinary memories and can retain the meaning as well as the sense of things.

## HAWTHORN
### *(May 13—June 9)*

To anyone who doesn't know them well, Hawthorn may seem matter-of-fact and practical . . . but deep down, they are wildly creative and even a little silly. They are powerfully curious, and this curiosity allows them to see the humor in most situations. They are adaptive and malleable—changeable as a chameleon on the outside, but true to themselves within.

## OAK

### *(June 10—July 7)*

Oak is a strong, fierce protector. They may find themselves working for causes that advance social justice or environmental protection. But their ferocity is tempered with gentleness and a sense of optimism about the world. They carry the weight of history and their ancestors, and this leads them to value family—chosen or otherwise—above all.

## HOLLY

### *(July 8—August 4)*

Holly is a natural leader due to their perseverance and dedication. They inspire others because they never, ever give up. Their innate intelligence and competitive nature drive their ambition, but they are also both kind and generous and care deeply about the people in their lives.

## HAZEL

### *(August 5—September 1)*

Hazel is organized, efficient, and extremely intelligent. They excel in academics and their analytical nature helps them make quick, smart decisions. They are drawn to science and want to understand and succeed in a number of different areas—from crafting to baking to astronomy.

## VINE

### *(September 2—September 29)*

Vine is deeply empathetic, and their ability to see another's perspective can cause them to have difficulty making decisions or choosing the right path. They can also appear unpredictable from the outside, as their intuitive nature may seem contradictory to others. They intensely enjoy the pleasures of life.

## IVY

### *(September 30—October 27)*

Ivy is loyal and loving, with a giving nature—they are always available to help or offer whatever support they can. When they are facing a difficulty, they have trouble asking for help, often enduring it in silence—but they have a strong sense of faith and optimism that everything will work out.

## REED

### *(October 28—November 23)*

Reed is thoughtful and occasionally secretive. They think deeply and want to know *why* the world is the way that it is. They would make a terrific historian, scientist, archaeologist, or journalist. They have a strong sense of the importance of truth.

## ELDER

### *(November 24—December 23)*

Elder is a free spirit, outspoken and creative. They are constantly seeking new experiences and new challenges. Despite their frank communication style, they are loving and generous and always willing to offer their plentiful support.

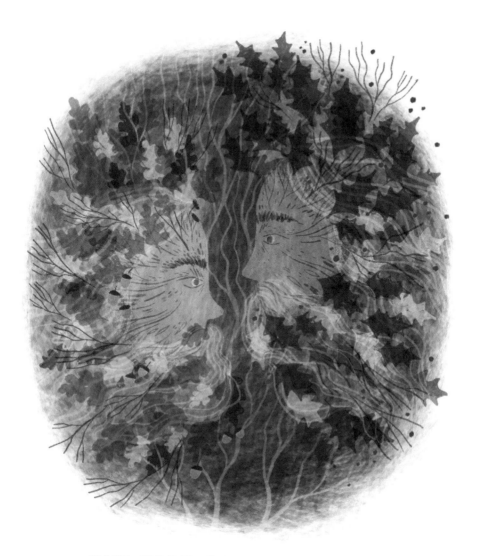

# THE TALE OF THE OAK KING
# AND THE HOLLY KING

Every culture around the world has a folkloric tradition that explains the Wheel of the Year—the shifting of the seasons round and round in an eternal cycle. In ancient Greece, Persephone, daughter of Demeter, the goddess of fertility and agriculture, is the goddess of spring and was beloved by Hades, lord of the Underworld. He took her to his land against her will—Greek legends were particularly objectionable in this regard—and her furious mother refused to allow any plants to grow until Persephone was returned to her. But Persephone had already consumed six seeds from a pomegranate, the fruit of the Underworld, which made her its queen. And so the goddess of spring spends half the year in the Underworld, and the world bursts back into life when she returns home.

In a remarkably similar Hopi story, Blue Corn Maiden was gathering firewood when she came upon the Winter Katsina, the spirit of winter. He fell in love with her and brought her to his home, keeping her there even after she longed to go home—much the way Hades held on to Persephone. But one day, Blue Corn Maiden dug her way out through the snow and lit a fire, melting a path that allowed the Summer Katsina to save her. Winter Katsina and Summer Katsina met in battle but quickly agreed that neither could be the victor, and Blue Corn Maiden agreed to spend half the year with Summer and half the year with Winter.

In pagan traditions, the spirit of summer known as the Oak King and the spirit of winter known as the Holly King do in fact engage in battle—and not over a comely maiden, either. They fight because they must, because they are each other's mirror and also each other's antithesis. And so, while one cannot exist without the other, they will always fight for supremacy, winning and then losing and then winning again, over and over forever.

The Oak King, ruler of the warmer, lighter months, represents growth and expansion. His half of the Wheel of the Year is a time to work and imagine. The possibilities he offers are endless, but they can also be cumbersome and eventually even exhausting.

There is, in all of these stories, a natural tendency to value warmth over cold and light over darkness. As the year fades, we can curse the simultaneous waning of the Oak King's powers. But the truth is, we need the rest the Holly King provides—no one can strive forever without respite. The time of the Holly King is a period of safety and restoration, when the world dreams and prepares for a new beginning.

And so, rather than holding a preference for one or the other, we can honor them both. We don't even need to think of them as enemies, locked in their eternal struggle for power. Instead, we can think of them as friends who play a pleasant and competitive game, knowing that they will each win, and lose, and win again—and whenever one succeeds the other, he provides us with the gifts we have been longing for in his absence.

PART 1

*the*

# OAK KING

# OAK KING EMBLEM

The Oak King is often associated with the Green Man, a fertility spirit who represents the growth of the forest. And really, what could be more ideal for your sacred grove? Carvings or other emblems of the Green Man have been found all over the world, in Iraq, Nepal, India, and from all over Europe, from as early as the second century

These emblems typically take three forms:

**THE FOLIATE HEAD, which is covered entirely in green leaves**

**THE DISGORGING HEAD, which expels vegetation from its mouth**

**THE BLOODSUCKER HEAD, which appears to have vegetation sprouting from its skull, including from its eyes, nose, mouth, and ears**

If all that sounds a little terrifying to you, you're not alone. A quick Google Images search for the Green Man will produce some fairly off-putting results, and there is absolutely no call for you to place a repugnant or otherwise unpleasant emblem in your haven of peace, magic, and creativity.

Instead, think about what the concept of the Oak King—and the Green Man—means to *you*—and consider how you can best craft or find that something that embodies that concept. Maybe that means wandering around your grove in search of a moss-covered rock or walking a nearby shore to find a piece of driftwood. Maybe it means painting something—it doesn't need to be a face, although it can be—and coating it in wax or laminating it so that it can withstand the elements. You could make a simple wood carving or work with clay. You could fashion sticks and leaves into a vaguely head-shaped sculpture.

*What* the emblem is doesn't actually matter all that much. What matters is the meaning you give it.

Once you have chosen your emblem, it's time to introduce it to your grove. You don't want to just hang a picture or place a statue without asking permission—and in fact, if your sacred grove is on public land, you may not be able to. In those cases, you will need to take your emblem with you when you go. This is not only absolutely fine, it's actually quite wonderful, as your emblem will allow you to bring the spirit of your sacred grove with you when you go—which may be useful when you are unable to visit in person.

It's best to select a location that will allow you to nestle your emblem either among the roots or on a branch of your tree—you don't want to hammer nails into part of your sacred grove. Once you've found a spot that feels right, bow your head, listening to the trees. When you sense their interest and acceptance, carefully and reverently place your emblem. This is your symbol of the Oak King, and it will rest here for half of the year, from the first whisper of spring to the final shout of summer. Visit it often.

# DAWN RITUAL

Dawn rituals are by nature drowsy affairs. The world is just waking up. Tempting as it may be to down a cup of coffee or tea before performing this ritual, try to restrain that impulse. It's okay to be sleepy. Allow yourself that sensation. Give yourself permission to move slowly, stumbling a little in the dark.

There's a heaviness to the light and the air that echoes the heaviness in your body. As difficult as it is for you to drag yourself out of bed, consider that it is as though the earth itself is struggling to shake off the weight of sleep.

In truth, that sensation of *thickness* in the air can feel almost oppressive . . . but then, the dawn breaks. It unleashes the wonder of the day. The sun rises and brings with it a burst of energy along with its burst of light.

Other rituals can be larger affairs, with special attire and a sense of ceremony. But this one in this gray half-light can be performed in your pajamas. It doesn't require much of you. In fact, it can be as simple as stepping outside and offering a sleepy wave to the emerging sun.

But if you feel called to do more, run the tips of your fingers along any blades of grass you see sparkling in this rarely witnessed slant of light. Let your eye catch upon a glistening spiderweb. Gather the dew, the wild water of the morning, and anoint yourself with it. Sweep it across your eyelids, your temples, the base of your throat, your breast.

René Daumal said, "Each time dawn appears, the mystery is there in its entirety." Consider—what is "the mystery" for you? What can you see in this most sacred light?

# IMBOLC

## *February 1*

Imbolc occurs on the day the first blush of spring enters the world. Sometimes referred to as St. Brigid's Day, it falls on the midpoint between the winter solstice (also known as Yule, or the day of the Holly King) and the spring equinox (also known as Ostara). Imbolc marks the beginning of the end of winter, the day on which the Oak King begins his rise.

Brigid, a Celtic goddess turned Catholic saint, rules over livestock. Think about that term *livestock* for a moment. These days, we think of smelly fields of cattle and pigs whose primary purpose in life is to become bacon. But once upon a time, it was understood on physical and spiritual levels that these animals provided *life,* and they were thus treated with the respect that such valuable resources deserved. They were cared for and treasured. A forest witch need not be vegan or vegetarian, but we all ought to live with that same respect for the creatures that sustain us.

Brigid also ruled over wisdom, poetry, healing, and protection—all attributes that resonate more with the resting time of the Holly King. It is almost as if her role is to carry those aspects forward into the time of the Oak King. Little dolls made out of corn husks left over from the harvest were known as Brideogs, and they serve as incarnations of Brigid for Imbolc. Brigid's crosses are made of rushes or dried grasses woven together and can be hung in your windows for protection.

Brigid was associated with clootie wells—sacred healing wells found across Celtic areas of Europe including Scotland, Cornwall, and Ireland. These wells were freshwater springs that burst forth from the base of a tree, most often a hawthorn or ash. When a person was in need of healing, they might take water from the well to wet a piece of cloth that they would use to anoint or wash the injured part of the body. They would then tie the cloth to a branch of the tree and sometimes would walk a circle around the well a sacred number of times—often a multiple of three or seven—before leaving an offering of a coin or a stone.

Making a pilgrimage to a clootie well is a traditional way to celebrate Imbolc, though of course those who live in other parts of the world must adapt their own version of this pilgrimage. You might consider researching the location of a nearby spring, brook, or pond—any form of wild water (aka water that hasn't been managed by humans) will do.

Choose your offering carefully. It doesn't need to be anything big or valuable; it simply must have meaning for *you*. Perhaps you'll offer a penny you found or a stone that feels good and right in your hand. You may want to leave a Brideog or a Brigid's cross as well. The cloth can be anything from a ribbon to a swatch of fabric—again, trust your intuition.

Your visit to a clootie well doesn't need to be for a physical ailment. You may wish to heal anxiety, hurt feelings, a relationship—even a broken heart.

(Depending on the location of your chosen well, you may want to remove your offering and clootie cloth at the end of your ritual. Don't worry—the meaning and magic of your interaction with the well will remain.)

## PLANTS THAT THRIVE NEAR IMBOLC

# BIRCH
### *Betula alba*

Beith, the birch tree, is the first to revive itself after a wildfire and the first to awaken after its winter sleep. The younger trees have thin, paperlike bark that peels off in sheets, and the sweet birch variety produces a root beer–like oil used to flavor birch beer. An infusion made from new leaves gathered in the spring can help to heal the dry, cracked skin of winter, and birch leaf tinctures or bitters can help with digestion. The terpenes (the compounds that produce scent in plants) of birch invite a sense of

rowan

elm

crocus

hellebore

winter aconite

snowdrop

birch

calm and well-being for many. Birch represents renewal and new beginnings, as well as protection and purification. Tying a red ribbon on a birch branch will cast a protection spell around you, and cradles made of birch will protect an infant from malevolent powers. Small birch branches or twigs carved with Ogham can be carried or hung for protection.

### SUGGESTED SPELL

**Gather a piece of cast-off birch bark. If you take it fresh from the tree, peel it off very gently, being careful not to disturb the darker, thicker bark underneath. Wash the bark gently with warm water and dish soap, then smooth it flat and allow it to dry. Once it's dry, you can write on it with your favorite pen—it doesn't require any kind of special ink. Consider this question: What do you want the birch to hold for you? You can write your intentions for a new beginning, or you can write your vulnerabilities—any areas in your life where you require additional protection. And often, you may feel called to write them both, as most of the time, they are intertwined.**

# CROCUS
*Crocus*

The snow crocus is one of the first flowers of the year to bloom. Crocuses contain powerful healing energy, and so you might drag the crocus blossom along any hurt you receive, helping to mend a sprain or speed the process of repair for a broken leg. Once upon a time in Ireland, bed linens were rinsed with crocus blossom water to promote strength and healing during sleep. Crocuses are symbolic of cheerfulness and particularly good for spells for new beginnings, love, friendship, peace, and divination.

## SUGGESTED SPELL

For divination work, pick a single crocus and gently hold it between the index finger and thumb of your nondominant hand. Move your fingers back and forth, rolling the stem. Stare into the center of the blossom as it spins, allowing your vision to blur and watching it like a rotating pinwheel. What do you see? If the crocus represents new beginnings, what is starting for you?

# ELM
## *Ulmus*

The elm, or Ailim, is one of the first trees to blossom, with its buds appearing as early as late January. It is said that fairies prefer it and will make their homes within its branches or beneath its roots. It is a protective tree, but also a loving one. Carrying bits of its bark will invite a warm, gentle love into your life. Because of its early return to the Oak King's world, the elm is also a tree of vision, offering clear sight and forethought.

## SUGGESTED SPELL

Take advantage of the elm's gift for long-term planning by bringing a piece of paper to a large tree. Run your palm over its bark, noting how rough and jagged—yet firm—it is. On your paper, write down a current goal you're working toward with as much detail as possible. Then place the paper against the bark, and use a crayon or soft pencil to create a rubbing, coloring the texture and energy of the elm over your writing—not obscuring it, but bringing elm's wisdom and ambition to it.

# HELLEBORE
## *Helleborus orientalis*

Also known as the winter rose, hellebore blooms in February, with some varieties continuing to blossom until Beltane in early May. This delicate, mysterious blossom dips its head toward the ground, as if bowing to the earth—perhaps because of its connections with the Underworld. Hellebore is particularly poisonous, and in ancient Greece, it was used to poison a besieged city's water supply . . . but it was also used to draw out madness caused by Dionysus, the god of revelry and excess. This gothic, shadowy flower thrives in the hard, frozen ground and is also said to have been beloved of the witches of yore. In fact, it is rumored to be one of the ingredients in flying ointment, as well as in a powder that, when walked upon, could make the caster of the spell invisible. It also provides protection and relieves anxiety—Victorian women would bring a vase full of hellebore into a room where people had been fighting so that the hellebore could disperse all the negative energy in the air.

### SUGGESTED SPELL

**Despite its rather dark history, hellebore is known for being a flower of hope . . . If we think about it for a moment, maybe that makes sense. It is only out of darkness that hope can arise—and it is amid darkness when hope is most needed. Since hellebore is so poisonous, it's actually best to leave it where it grows. (If you do pick it, make sure to wear gloves.) If you can, cast this spell just before the dawn, sitting beside the blossom. Take a piece of paper and a pencil and write down all your worries, all that has gone wrong. This may be painful, but let it all come out. Once you've finished, rub your fingers in the dirt beside the hellebore, and use that soil to smudge away the pencil marks, blurring them. Cover the whole sheet of paper with dirt if you like, then dust it off. The stains will**

remain, and you can choose to tuck the paper into your pocket or leave it on your altar as a reminder that hellebore's hopeful energy is guiding you forward, through the cold, hard ground of your struggles, to bloom in the dawning light.

# ROWAN
## *Sorbus*

Luis, or rowan, is a shrublike tree often adorned with bloodred berries. These berries, while acidic and slightly bitter, can be made into jams or used to brew tinctures or cordials. The rowan is a highly protective tree, said to shield the bearer from anything from fairies to witches to storms. If you spotted someone dancing in a fairy ring, you could safely pull them out by offering them a rowan branch to hold. Rowan is also known as the "wayfarer's tree," as it would provide guidance to those who are lost. These days, it serves as a portal between the known and the unknown; sitting beneath its branches can give you access to insights and understandings you may not have realized you possessed. A rowan is itself a liminal space—a threshold between what you know and what you only *think* you know.

## SUGGESTED SPELL
After asking the tree's permission, cut two small twigs from its branches, or better still, gather some twigs that have already fallen on the ground. Sit beneath the tree, and using red string or yarn, create a Brigid's cross with the twigs, winding the string around and over and between the twigs until they are secure. With each wrap, murmur "protect" as you spin the doll round and round. Tie off the string, and hang your rowan cross over your threshold at home, to protect your own liminal space.

# SNOWDROP
## *Galanthus nivalis*

*Galanthus* means "milk flower" in Greek, and the snowdrop is called thus for its faint, sweet, milky-almond scent. Another charming name for the snowdrop is "February Fairmaids," perhaps a reference to an old German tale in which the then-colorless snow begged the flowers to share their color. All the flowers refused, greedily hoarding their reds, pinks, blues, and oranges. But the humble snowdrop, quiet and small, offered to share, and so the snow and the snowdrop blend into one another. These flowers are often a little unbalanced, with an uneven number of segments, making them somewhat less aesthetically pleasing than other blossoms. And yet, we can appreciate them all the more for their imperfections and their variability—not to mention their ease of propagation and growth. Snowdrops are particularly effective when used in spells for friendship, consolation, self-love, memory, hope, and kindness.

## SUGGESTED SPELL

Gather a small bouquet of snowdrops and bring them home with you, placing them in a vase or glass. Rest them on your altar or somewhere else where you will notice them often. Pay attention to them. How is each flower different from the others? Inhale their faint, kindhearted scent. Notice how your love for them does not diminish because of any of their perceived "imperfections." Let them be an example for you, and feel and express love for your own variability, foibles, and blemishes.

# WINTER ACONITE
## *Eranthis hyemalis*

Also known as winter wolf's bane, winter aconite is actually *not* related to aconite (also known as monkshood or wolfsbane) and is not as poisonous—but it's definitely not edible, either. It is, however, of vast importance to bees, given its early appearance—as a result, early honey harvests where winter aconite grows will give energy and promote healing. This sweet flower first became popular in the 1700s, when Lancelot "Capability" Brown, the famous landscape designer, started planting it in all the most fashionable country estates. This early fame makes this sweet, unassuming blossom surprisingly good for prosperity or manifestation spellwork.

## SUGGESTED SPELL

**Gather winter aconite in mid- to late morning, when the sun is high but still rising. Pluck a handful of blossoms, and float them in a small bowl or cup of water, watching them twist and sail like little boats. Gently place a droplet of water in each little yellow cup, setting an intention for healing and energy with each drop. For added benefit, consume a teaspoon of local honey.**

# OSTARA

### *The Spring Equinox*

While tales vary, a seasonally accurate depiction of the conflict between the Oak King and the Holly King declares that their battles take place on the two equinoxes—when the length of the day is equal to the length of the night and the two kings are fully in balance. Of course, one must always win, and so on Ostara, the Oak King defeats the Holly King.

Ostara, or Alban Eilir, celebrates another deity as well: Eostre, the Germanic goddess of spring and fertility. According to some legends— and it's difficult to trace how far back they actually go—Eostre sent a bird to spread word of spring across the lands. But her winged messenger could not survive in the harsh winter of the north and returned to her frozen and near death. Eostre saved the bird, transforming it into a furred creature with strong hind legs that could carry it for vast distances and at great speed, long ears that could sense any predator, and an ability to reproduce at alarmingly high rates—a trait suitable for a goddess of fertility. In gratitude, the creature that had once been a bird dotted the land with brightly colored eggs, heralding the return of spring.

So, if you've always wondered how rabbits who lay eggs came to be associated with Easter, there's your answer.

To celebrate the balance between light and dark—along with the knowledge that, henceforth, light will rule supreme—invite the spirit of Eostre into your sacred grove by hanging eggs from the branches of trees. Set an intention with each egg that you hang—for fertility (which can also be for creativity), for prosperity, for growth, and for a new beginning.

## BLOWN EGGS

Take an egg—or eggs, however many you want to make—and shake it. Put some energy into this! You want to break up the yolk and membranes. Using a pair of sharp-pointed scissors or a craft knife, pierce a small hole into both the top and bottom of your egg(s). Insert a toothpick or wooden skewer into the egg and move it up and down, twisting it around, smoothing out the holes.

Lift one of the holes to your lips and blow into it, using your breath to push the egg out through the other hole. (You'll want to have a bowl ready to catch it—you've got prescrambled egg coming your way!) Keep at it until the egg is completely emptied.

Rinse it off and dry it—and then decorate it! You can use food coloring or Easter egg dyes, or you might consider natural dyes.

# NATURALLY DYED EGGS

The formula for dyeing eggs with ordinary foodstuffs is as follows:

**CHOPPED PURPLE CABBAGE** = blue on white eggs, green on brown eggs

**RED ONION SKINS** = lavender on white eggs, red on brown eggs

**YELLOW ONION SKINS** = orange on white eggs, rusty red on brown eggs

**SHREDDED BEETS** = pink on white eggs, maroon on brown eggs

To make a batch of dye, add a one-to-one ratio of water and dyestuffs to a pot; so, for one cup water, add one cup of onions skins, etc. Bring the water to a boil and let it simmer, covered, for thirty minutes. Remove from the heat and let it cool. Strain out the dyestuffs, then stir in one tablespoon of white vinegar for every cup of water you used. Add the eggs, making sure they are completely submerged. (Be careful if you're using blown eggs, as they are quite fragile. This method also works quite well with hard-boiled eggs.) Let them soak overnight in the refrigerator.

## PLANTS THAT THRIVE NEAR OSTARA

# ALDER
### *Alnus*

By the time of Ostara, Fearn, the alder tree, is flourishing. It dwells on riverbanks, with its roots driving deep into the water. In fact, alderwood that has been submerged in water for a period of time does not rot, but instead grows even stronger. The alder is said to be a portal tree, allowing access to the fairy realms—or, more practically, access to another perspective or way of viewing a situation. Alder is said to be protected by water spirits, but its branches can be used to make whistles that call on the spirits of air. Alder is also a very protective tree, offering shelter and safety in times of danger. You can harness that safety by gathering alder wands, or twigs, and using them as protective charms.

### SUGGESTED SPELL

To make your own alder wand, collect a twig—after first asking permission, of course—that matches the length from your elbow to the tips of your fingers. Using a small knife, scrape away the bark, always scraping away from your body. (If you like, you can also leave some bark in place for a more gnarled-looking wand.) With the knife, carefully round the ends of the wand so they aren't sharp. From there, add whatever personal touches you like. You might consider etching a sigil into the wand or wrapping the base of it with string or yarn—black is typically a protective color, or you might choose white for cleansing. You could also glue on a protective crystal, like black tourmaline, smoky quartz, or obsidian.

*alder*

*daffodil*

*cherry*

*gorse*

*mint*

*cyclamen*

*ash*

# ASH
## *Fraxinus excelsior*

In Norse mythology, Yggdrasil, the world tree, was an enormous ash, known as Nion in Ogham. Its roots were watered in the underworld by the Norns (i.e., the Fates), and its branches stretched across all the world, even reaching the arc of the heavens. Ash is associated with growth and also with the sea, as a cross carved of ash wood could protect the bearer from drowning. In fact, any object or tool made from ash is said to be more durable, and more productive, than the same object made from any other wood; spears—like Odin's, which was carved from Yggdrasil—could fly farther, axes would remain sharper, and tables would bear greater feasts.

## SUGGESTED SPELL

**Visit an ash tree and, after asking its permission, collect some of its leaves. Bring them home, and scatter some (use a multiple of three) at each of the four corners of your property or home—the spirit of the ash will keep you safe. While you're at it, place some ash leaves beneath your pillow and sleep atop them—they might give you prophetic dreams.**

# CHERRY
## *Prunus*

When the first cherries begin to blossom on the archipelago, the Japan Meteorological Agency tracks the *sakura zensen,* or the path of the cherries as they spread their bloom of color across the country. Their transience, along with their beauty, have for eons represented the ephemeral nature of life—we are all here only for a brief time. How much beauty can we pour into our lives in the time that we do have? In a lovely symbolic connection, cherries also represent love, and it is said that if you tie a strand of your hair on the branch of a blossoming cherry tree, love will soon make its way to you.

## SUGGESTED SPELL

**Sit or lie beneath a blossoming cherry tree and practice** *hanami,* **the Japanese art of flower viewing. You can do this alone or with friends, and even have a picnic complete with beverages—if you can source some cherry wine or sake, all the better! This is meant to be fun and pleasurable . . . but while you're there, take a quiet moment to brush your fingertips across the petals of a blossom that speaks to you. In gratitude for its presence and in honor of its brief stay, set an intention for how you will seek out beauty—whatever that means to you.**

# CYCLAMEN
## *Cyclamen coum*

Cyclamen's waxy blossoms grow low to the ground, often shaded beneath the trees, making them ideal additions to any sacred grove. Oddly, this sweet little flower—known for its ability to produce feelings of happiness, creativity, protection, and love—was once used to send a message of resigned farewell in the Victorian language of flowers. Perhaps it was a way of bidding goodbye to the Holly King's season of protection? In any case, cyclamen is sacred to Hecate, the goddess of witches, and as such will boost the power of any spell you choose. However, it is particularly effective in love spells; if you want to bring a little more joy to a relationship, cyclamen is quite helpful.

Together with the person or persons you love (and remember, this can be any kind of love—familial, romantic, or the love between friends), gather cyclamen in some multiple of three that can also be divided by the number of people included in the spell. (So if there are two of you, gather six blossoms, if there are three of you, gather nine blossoms, etc.). Stand facing each other, with each person holding their share of flowers. One by one, exchange flowers, and with each exchange, imbue the blossom with your feelings of love for the other person. If you want, you can speak these thoughts aloud, sharing something in particular that you love about them. When the exchange is complete, each person should take their new, gifted flowers and keep them close.

# DAFFODIL
## *Narcissus*

Wordsworth described daffodils as "jocund company," and so they are—buttery yellow sprites that herald the coming sunshine. Wearing a daffodil in your breast pocket will invite good luck, and daffodils are best used in spells for happiness, self-love, forgiveness, truth, creativity, rebirth, and new beginnings.

Whenever you, like Wordsworth, are feeling "lonely as a cloud," turn to the daffodil. Its friendly, open face with its silly shaped corona is almost like a puppy—you can even "boop" it if you like. Press your nose against the corona, inhaling and exhaling, exchanging its breath for yours. Sit with it in bright light—sunshine if possible, or under a lamp if not—and stare at it, memorizing its shape and color. Look at it for so long that, when you close your eyes, you can see the reversed image of the daffodil against your eyelids. It will accompany you throughout your day, in your heart and your mind.

# GORSE
## *Ulex*

The spiny Onn, or gorse, is sometimes known as furze. It flowers by Ostara, with golden blossoms peeking through its prickles. It is a determined plant, and its protective nature can keep out anything from fairies to farm predators to harmful energies. Gorse, being a hardy and fairly invasive low-growing shrub, will persevere against whatever stands in its way.

### SUGGESTED SPELL

Gorse's energy is best used in prosperity or manifestation spells, as it will urge you onward toward your desires. When it's in bloom (and it usually is—there are always at least a few flowers present, no matter the season), gather a quarter cup's worth of flowers, concentrating on what you want to manifest as you pick. When you get home, set a pot of water on to boil. When it is hot, add your flowers, letting them simmer for ten minutes or so. Strain out your tea, and as you sip it, let gorse guide you in writing down a simple to-do list. What have you been avoiding? Gorse will help you take that next step.

# MINT
## *Mentha*

According to Greek mythology, before it was a plant, Mintha was a nymph who loved Hades. But when Hades fell in love with and kidnapped Persephone, Mintha despaired and claimed in her jealousy that she was more beautiful than Persephone anyway. This did not sit well with Demeter, Persephone's loving mother, and she trampled Mintha beneath her bare feet. However, it doesn't seem to have done mint any harm. It grows in abundance, low to the ground perhaps, but always making its presence known with its sharp, refreshing scent. Mint is particularly good for abundance, luck, healing, and love spells.

### SUGGESTED SPELL

Mint is a powerful energizer, offering clarity of thought—even wisdom. Gather a generous handful of fresh mint, wild grown if you can find it, and wash it well. Tear the leaves or bruise them in a mortar and pestle, add them to a small jar, and then cover them in vodka. Let the mixture steep for at least two weeks, and then consume a teaspoon of this tincture whenever you need a burst of fresh, new thinking. A tincture is a concentrated potion; just a small amount is extremely potent.

# MIDDAY RITUAL

Noon is the time of the Oak King. We are closest to the sun and can stand with little to no shadow beneath its bright gaze. Even on cloudy days when we cannot see it clearly, the sun's light is still there.

Of course, noon considered this way, as when the sun is at its zenith, does not necessarily mean when the clock is exactly at 12. Just as the calendar of trees does not follow the Gregorian months, neither does the sun obey the strict rules of Daylight Savings Time. On the day you want to perform this ritual, look up online exactly what time the sun will be at its zenith. Then be ready to perform this ritual at that time, gathering everything you will need in advance.

Of course, all a spell or ritual ever *really* requires is you and your intentions—but you can help ground and boost those intentions with a few supplies.

- **Sunstone, peridot, or pyrite**
- **Marigold, chamomile, or sunflower**

Find a place to sit on the earth in direct sunlight—wearing sunscreen, of course! Hold your chosen crystal in your nondominant hand and your flower in the other. Close your eyes, and lift your face to the sun.

Feel the sun's warmth on your face, and see its bright light against your eyelids. Inhale that brightness, that shining gift of life and warmth. Exhale your own warmth in return.

Feel the energies of the very different elements in your hands. One is hard, while the other is malleable. And yet, they are both of the earth and both symbolic of the sun. Let their complementary energies intermingle within you. Consider these questions: Where in your life should you be firm and fiery like the sun? And where in your life should you bend and shift with the breeze, following the light?

# BELTANE

## *May 1*

Beltane occurs at the height of spring and fertility—and so it is often a bit of a bacchanal. Indeed, its roots are in Maiouma (also known as the Roman Floralia), an ancient festival dedicated to Dionysus and Aphrodite. It is also a night for witches—in Germany, Beltane was known as Walpurgisnacht; in Bavaria it is Hexennacht; and in Portugal, it is Dia das Bruxas. In the German tradition, on this night witches would gather on the Brocken, the highest peak in the Harz Mountains, to cast their most powerful spells—the ones that required a full coven.

Bonfires lit on this night provide protection from witches, or even fairies. But, for the brave, leaping over a bonfire will secure a year of good luck and bounty—as if by leaning into your fear, you secure your own, more lasting protection. Other Beltane practices for protection include warding off fairies by offering them libations of milk; placing three black coals under a butter churn; and hanging branches of hawthorn from milk pails, around the barn, and from cows' tails to prevent the milk from going sour.

Farmers would then lead a procession around the boundaries of the property, bearing with them their seeds, tools, and water drawn from the well. They would pause at the northernmost point, then the easternmost, the southernmost, and the westernmost. At each pause they would scatter vervain for additional protection.

It wasn't all fear and solemnity, though—maidens would rise with the dawn on Beltane and bathe their faces with the morning dew, allowing them to dry in the still-chilly air. They might also collect the dew in a jar to rest in the sunlight, using it throughout the year to increase beauty and general desirability. As the saying goes, *I wash my face in water that has never rained nor run and dry it in a towel that was never wove nor spun.*

Folklorist Alexander Carmichael learned the following Scottish Gaelic Beltane Blessing from a crofter. A verse of it translates to:

*Everything within my dwelling or in my possession*
*All kine and crops, all flocks and corn*
*From Hallow Eve to Beltane Eve*
*With goodly progress and gentle blessing*
*From sea to sea, and every river mouth*
*From wave to wave, and base of waterfall*

For your own Beltane celebration, you may wish to follow all of the above traditions, though perhaps you might skip tying branches to cows' tails, and for safety reasons it's probably best not to try jumping over a fire. But there is another Beltane custom that translates particularly well to forest magic—the making of a May Bough.

You'll want to start by selecting a relatively sizable branch in your sacred grove, as this will be your May Bough. Begin to decorate it with yellow and white flowers you have gathered, including primrose, chamomile, and hawthorn—which is made easier and lovelier if you've first strung the flowers together into a garland. It is traditional to decorate the bough with candles, but you're likely better off using a string of battery-powered LED lights, which serve the same intention of light and goodwill. If you have any leftover flowers, take them home with you when you go, scattering them across your doorstep as an invitation of hope and protection.

## PLANTS THAT THRIVE NEAR BELTANE

## ASPEN
### *Populus tremula*

Eadhadh, or aspen, is about success through endurance. Like most deciduous trees, aspens drop their leaves in winter, but their bark is photosynthetic, so they are able to continue growing and thriving even in the snow—and they can survive forest fires, as well. They grow in large colonies derived from a single seed—as if acres and acres of aspen were one single organism. In fact, one such aspen colony in Utah is thought to

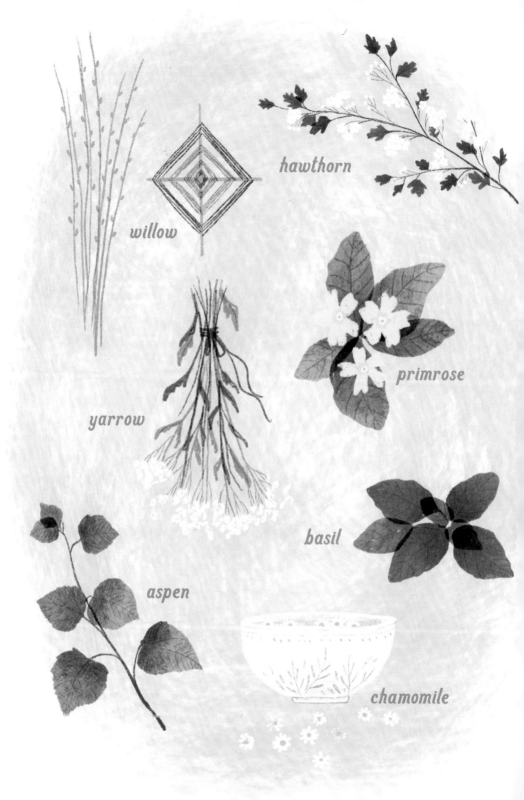

willow

hawthorn

primrose

yarrow

basil

aspen

chamomile

be 80,000 years old. Because of their enduring vision, they are able to enhance psychic ability.

**Lie beneath an aspen tree and watch its leaves tremble against the sky. They flutter with the slightest breeze, delicate despite the tree's strength of will. Let that hypnotic dance lull you and allow your mind to drift. What can you see in those flickers of green and yellow? Aspen's gift is endurance but also malleability—what is changing in you, as you adapt to your ever-shifting life?**

# BASIL

## *Ocimum basilicum*

Basil is a contradictory herb. In some cultures, it is viewed as a force for good, while in others it is perceived in quite a negative light. For example, ancient Greeks believed that basil was a symbol of hate, misfortune, and poverty—but in the West Indies, basil arranged around a shop will attract customers. These days, the positive aspects of basil have taken precedence; it is a symbol of love and goodwill, and giving a basil plant to a newlywed or partnered couple will convey your intentions for the success of their relationship. Basil gives you strength, allowing you to move forward in spite of any fears or doubts.

**If you are in the midst of a disagreement with someone you love, turn to basil for assistance. This can be as simple as diffusing some basil essential oil—the scent alone can help you see the other person's point of view and vice versa. If they are amenable, however, you can carry this a bit**

further by taking a basil leaf and placing it against your heart, setting your intention to listen and allowing your love for the other person to enter the leaf. When you've finished, offer the leaf to them to place to their heart in turn.

# CHAMOMILE
## *Anthemis nobilis*

Chamomile, when planted in a garden, will strengthen the other plants it is nestled with—that is how powerful this calming and healing herb can be. Chamomile is perfect for magic that involves the sun, particularly the kind that evokes warm, lazy days lying beneath tree branches or watching the clouds pass overhead. It is a flower of friendship, love, tranquility, and luck, and it will protect you from negativity, clearing away anything you are carrying that you no longer need.

## SUGGESTED SPELL

If you feel you've been carrying an excessive amount of emotional weight, take a ritual chamomile bath. Sprinkle fresh or dried chamomile blossoms—or a combination of the two!—into hot water. If you have a bath that you can immerse your entire body in, great, but if not, you can simply bathe your face, either by splashing the chamomile water with your hands or pouring the bowl over your head, rinsing all that negative energy away.

# HAWTHORN
## *Crataegus monogyna*

Hawthorn goes by a variety of names, including Huath, mayflower, thorn apple, and Glastonbury Thorn, and when it grows near oak and ash, the three are said to be a gathering place for the fae, who may even be visible to human folk. It is also said that on Walpurgisnacht, the witches who roam may turn into hawthorn trees. Hawthorn is by all accounts a force for protection and creativity; sprigs of hawthorn placed around the home will keep malicious forces from entering, and hawthorn placed beneath a bed may invite conception.

### SUGGESTED SPELL

**Make a tincture of hawthorn using the leaves and flowers, as on page 26. In this case, you'll let the tincture steep longer—for several months, in fact. In the fall, when the fruits of the tree—known as hawthorn hips, much like rose hips—are ripe, harvest them. You'll want to simmer them for about thirty minutes, then press them through a strainer, squeezing out the juice. Strain out your reserved tincture and add it to the juice—this tart, bright potion will give you a creative burst whenever you require it.**

# PRIMROSE
## *Primula vulgaris*

Primrose is said to attract fairies—which is interesting, since many of the plants and rituals we've discussed are renowned for their ability to protect *against* the fae. To understand this dichotomy and why Celtic folklore seems to both value and fear fairies, it's useful to think of them as an embodiment of nature. As forest witches, we not only appreciate and respect nature, we also revere and even worship it. We know what it has to offer us, and what we owe it in return. And yet, that reverence is tempered with rational unease; nature can be dangerous, even harmful—and that was especially true in the days before the Industrial Revolution. But primrose is for the times when you feel most at ease with nature and recognize it as a force that protects, rather than endangers.

## SUGGESTED SPELL

**Collect three primrose blossoms, preferably early in the morning when the dew is still upon them. Brush your cheeks with their dew, blessing and anointing yourself. Take them home and rest them on a windowsill to dry and serve as an invitation for the fairies. When they have dried, but before they have begun to wilt, carefully place them between two pieces of paper and weight them down with a couple of heavy books. Let them rest there for a week until they have preserved fully. Then you can add them to your altar, paste them onto cardstock and seal them with Mod Podge, or whatever works best for you as a way to keep their hopeful, reverent nature close.**

# WILLOW
## *Salix*

Saille, or willow, is known for its sheltering branches—which are like a peaceful dome you can lie beneath—and also its malleability. It is used to make living arches and trellises—even sculptures. It is a powerfully healing plant; in fact, willow bark can be used to make a pain-relieving tea. It promotes growth, not just magically but literally. When you take the cuttings of a young willow tree and soak them in water for a time, this "willow water" can be used to help other plants take root. The willow is nurturing and kind, sharing its intuitive, feminine wisdom.

## SUGGESTED SPELL

Gather a bundle of soft, pliable willow shoots or branches. Allow them to dry for a full lunar cycle, then soak them in water for three nights, until they are flexible once more. At this point, you can weave anything you like, but to make a traditional cross or an Ojos de Dios (God's Eye), take two sturdy branches (they don't have to be willow) and lay them crosswise. Take a willow shoot and wind it across and around, forming an X and joining the branches together. Depending on how large you want your cross to be, you may need to add more willow shoots as you go. Tie off with string if necessary, and hang your cross where it can watch over you.

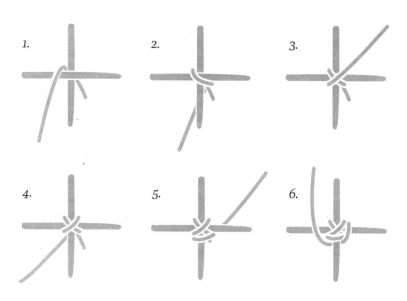

# YARROW
## *Achillea millefolium*

Also known as woundwort, seven year's love, bad man's plaything, eerie, and devil's nettle, yarrow is a profoundly powerful plant. While it is poisonous to consume in large amounts, when used in a tea it can provide courage, healing, and protection—Achilles used it to staunch the wounds of his men during the Trojan War. It can even enhance psychic ability, and dried yarrow stalks are traditionally used to throw the I Ching.

### SUGGESTED SPELL

Gather yarrow that has just begun to droop and hang it upside down to dry. You can leave it hanging for a general protection, healing, or love spell—it will place a blessing over your house. When you need it, harvest the dried flowers, gathering a teaspoon's worth, and crumble them with a mortar and pestle while putting a pot of water on to boil. Steep your yarrow for ten minutes, surrounding it with agate, amethyst, aquamarine, blue lace agate, calcite, fluorite, lapis lazuli, opal, or tigereye crystals. Prepare this tea whenever you need to divine your own inner truth.

# LITHA

## *The Summer Solstice*

On this day, the Oak King reaches the height of his powers. They will begin to wane from this moment forth, but for now, at this instant of the longest day and the shortest night, the Oak King reigns supreme. The world is at its most bountiful—green and blossoming, without the summer heat. Perhaps that is why June is the most popular month for weddings, for the creation of something new and fruitful.

Celebrations of Litha typically include some form of honey, as the bees have now wakened entirely and are working hard to ensure a good harvest. You might consider purchasing some mead (honey wine) or even brewing some yourself, though that would require some advance planning.

If you're feeling ambitious, brew your own mead! To do so, heat a half gallon of water until it is warm but not boiling, then stir in two pounds of honey. (Yes, mead requires a lot of honey!) Add the honey water mixture to a gallon jug with an airlock, then supplement your mead with any flavorings you like—you might consider herbs that are sacred to Litha, like lavender and rose, or some apple juice, grapes, or orange slices—whatever you want! Top off your mead with water until you have only two to three inches of room in your container. Add a half package of champagne yeast, then seal the jug tightly. Shake it *hard* for several minutes, then unscrew the top and seal it with the airlock. You'll see bubbles begin to form as the fermentation process begins.

From there, you can allow your mead to rest for about six weeks, or until the bubbles have subsided. Decant the mead into jars, leaving the sediment that gathers in the bottom of the jug. Let your mead age for several months, or even up to a year or two.

Everyone likes a good bonfire party, so if you're not too exhausted after your Beltane bacchanal, consider hosting another for Litha. If you are able to burn oak wood, you can release the Oak King's spirit into the night, scattering some lavender, rose, parsley, sage, and thyme over the flames and pouring a libation of mead for good measure.

If you're up for it, you can even keep the fire going all night—it is the shortest night of the year, after all—to symbolically carry the sun to the next dawn. Even the most raucous celebrations tend to die down in the moments before sunrise, so those last few hours could be a time of quiet contemplation and meditation. When at last the fire goes out and has cooled completely, save a handful of ashes in a jar and either scatter them in your garden or bring them to your sacred grove.

There are so many ways to celebrate Litha, but perhaps the most important is to spend some time with the Oak King. Make sure to visit your sacred grove on this day. Lie back and watch the flickering sunlight between the branches and leaves above you. Think of it like a secret Morse code only you can comprehend. What can you interpret? What message does your sacred grove have to offer?

## PLANTS THAT THRIVE NEAR LITHA

# FERN
### *Pteridophyta*

Also known as Devil Brushes, ferns grow in the secret places of the forest. Tucked away as they are into the understory, ferns are a little mysterious. They are said to bestow the power of invisibility if you carry them in your pocket, and sometimes ferns may take revenge on a traveler who treads upon them by leading them astray. These ancient plants do seem to carry knowledge that they do not always care to share—their mysteries are their own. But they provide shelter and protection, and because of their ability to bring the rain, they also have cleansing properties. Today we know that ferns reproduce through spores. Long ago, though, it was thought that their seeds were well-nigh invisible and dangerous to collect—but all the more powerful because of that. In fact, there was a legend that told of a mysterious fern blossom that bloomed for only one night—on Litha.

## SUGGESTED SPELL

**After asking permission, gently pull up a small fern plant directly from its forest or park home, keeping its roots intact. Carefully place it in a glass jar surrounded with moss that you have also collected and sprinkle it with water. Poke some holes in the top of the jar to allow air to flow, then seal the jar, creating a small terrarium. Place the jar somewhere out of direct sunlight, keeping it close so that your fern guide can offer its wisdom as it chooses.**

# HEATHER
### *Calluna vulgaris*

Uhr, or heather, that quintessential plant of the misty moors, stood as witness to the passions of Heathcliff. Queen Victoria watched as John Brown, the Scottish man rumored to be her lover after Prince Albert died, jumped out of their carriage to pick a sprig of white heather to bring her luck. Heather is also protective, sheltering the many wild beasties that run through its branches, and possesses soothing healing powers.

## SUGGESTED SPELL

Gather a large handful of heather blossoms, collecting the tiny flowers in a glass jar. Leave the jar open overnight, surrounded by rose quartz and aventurine. In the morning, dip your fingertips into the jar, lifting a few grains of heather and letting them fall. Set your intentions for luck, love, and gentle healing of the soul. When you're ready, step outside and stand facing the sun. Dipping your fingers into the jar once more, gather a small handful of heather and scatter it to the wind, letting heather take your wishes out into the world. Repeat until the jar is empty.

# LAVENDER
### *Lavandula angustifolia*

Lavender is renowned for its calming properties. Its delicate scent offers a soothing kind of protection, dispelling anxiety gently rather than shoving it away. In fact, this magical clearing of the internal cobwebs can make you more able to see the unseen, whether through inviting prophetic dreams or by inducing visions during meditation. It is an herb of peace, love, and kindness.

## SUGGESTED SPELL

To invite a vision, begin by collecting some dried lavender—if you have fresh lavender, it will dry quickly if hung upside down for a week or two. Bruise it slightly with a mortar and pestle. If you like, you can add mugwort or calendula, which are also powerful boosters of psychic ability. Heat some water to just boiling, then put your herbs in a tea strainer and allow them to steep for at least ten minutes. When your tea is cool enough to drink, sit comfortably. Close your eyes and inhale the steam, then exhale it back out. Repeat three times before

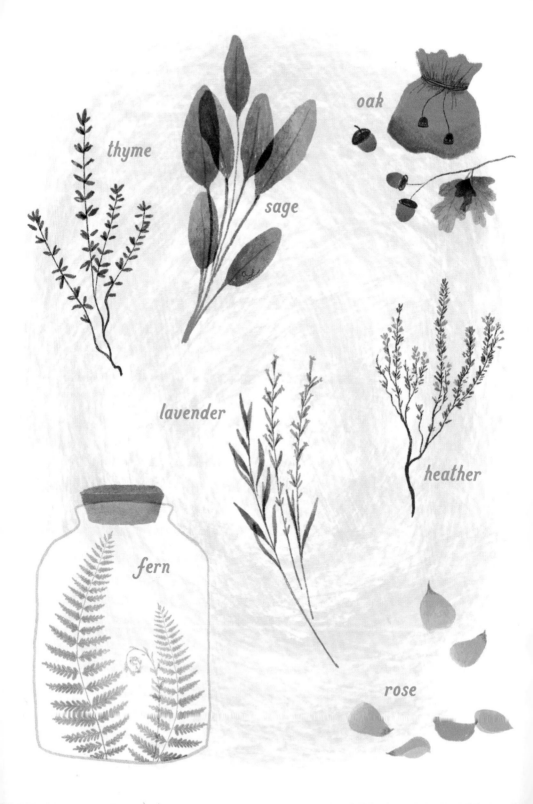

thyme

sage

oak

lavender

heather

fern

rose

taking your first sip. Then, drink your tea mindfully, paying attention to the flavors, the scents, and the sensations it provokes in your body. When your mind begins to wander, let it follow its own paths. See where it leads.

# OAK
## *Quercus*

Duir, the oak, has long been revered, even worshipped for its powerful strength and protective magic. Its solemn, responsible nature intertwines with its playfulness, in the way its leaves catch the wind and its acorn caps serve as fairy teacups or hats—and so it also provides a profound boost to creativity, wealth, longevity, and luck. Catching a falling oak leaf before it hits the ground ensures good health for a year—it's harder to do than you might think—and carrying an acorn in your pocket will offer you protection and a fertile imagination.

## SUGGESTED SPELL

While acorns typically don't fall until early autumn, you can always find a few scattered around beneath an oak tree. Take a walk one sunny afternoon and gather a few. Sort through what you've found, choosing one that best suits your needs. Do you want one with the cap attached, for additional protection, or open, to allow the flow of new ideas? Do you want one that is full and round, or more compact? Once you've chosen your acorn and decided on your intentions for it, cut a four-by-four-inch piece of fabric, and in the center of the cloth place the acorn as well as any crystals for protection (like obsidian or smoky quartz), creativity (like agate or carnelian), or wealth and longevity (like aventurine or jade). Add any herbs you like, then tie your fabric up with a piece of string. You can place this spell bag beneath your pillow or carry it with you wherever you go.

# ROSE
## *Rosa*

While individual rose varieties and colors all have their own meanings, a rose in general simply means love—of all kinds, in all forms. It can signify love for a friend, a romantic partner, a child—even love for one-self. Roses are also known for their fairy magic, as the fae are drawn to their beauty. And of course, the rose is renowned for its distinctive scent, which is deep and complex and always recognizable.

### SUGGESTED SPELL

There are so many ways to work with roses, whether by taking a bath with floating petals, sending a bouquet to a loved one (a magical spell in itself), or using dried roses to flavor food. But a simple way to incorporate rose magic into your repertoire is to brew your own rose water potion. You'll need a quarter cup of dried rose petals, or a cup of fresh, and a cup and a half of water. Put them in a pot and bring to a low boil. Simmer until all of the color has faded from the petals, then allow the mixture to cool. Strain out the petals and return them to the earth, storing the rose water in a dark glass bottle. You can spritz it on your face when you need a little love, add it to just about any beverage, or simply spray it into the air.

# SAGE
## *Salvia officinalis*

The Romans believed that sage was so powerful, it could create life—and yet, it would only grow in gardens tended by women. It is protective, cleansing, and helpful in both success and manifestation spells. But what sage is best known for is its wisdom: sage can help you not only know something, but understand it deeply. Consider sage the difference between intelligence and true wisdom—it invites the weight of experience and emotional understanding.

### SUGGESTED SPELL

**If you are struggling with a complex issue and require sage's assistance, take a fresh sage leaf and carefully inscribe your intentions on it with a needle. You can do this through a sigil you've created beforehand—a sigil is a symbol of a spell—or by using a single simple word. Place the leaf beneath your pillow and sleep on it for three nights. The sage will whisper to you in your dreams.**

# THYME
## *Thymus vulgaris*

Knights riding off to the Crusades would receive scarves embroidered with thyme to keep them safe. During periods of the year when thyme was more readily available, it was simply carried fresh in a pocket or worn pinned to the breast. Like roses, it also attracts fairies, for it is said that they love to dance among its leaves and blossoms. Thyme is a friendly, gentle herb, inviting strength and courage, as well as good health and simple pleasures.

## SUGGESTED SPELL

When you think about the idea of seeing fairies, what does that mean to you? For some, it may mean genuinely casting your eyes upon the fae. For others, it may mean becoming more aware of the unknown and unseen powers of this world, embracing the natural magic that is our daily life. Given the stresses of the everyday, sometimes that magic can be just as difficult to see as winged creatures or elven folk. When you've begun to feel blinded to forest magic, call upon thyme. Carry it with you like the knights of yore.

PART 2
*the*
# HOLLY KING

# HOLLY KING EMBLEM

If the Oak King can be compared to the Green Man, then the Holly King's counterpart is the Horned God. The Horned God is the male counterpart to Wicca's Threefold Goddess of the Maiden, Mother, and Crone. He rules over the wilderness, creativity, and the hunt.

The Horned God is simply an aspect of the Green Man—just as the Oak King and Holly King are complementary aspects—with a wilder flavor. The time of the Green Man/Oak King is one of cultivation and fruitful labor. But the coming of winter's chill heralds the arrival of the Horned God/Holly King, when labor cedes to rest, but also when cultivation is no longer available and we must turn to the hunt.

These days, of course, we are not reliant on foraging and trapping to supplement the year's harvest. But we can think of the wilderness and the hunt metaphorically—what wildness can we bring into our lives? What can we choose to seek with thought and careful preparation? Consider your intentions for the next half of the year as you create your emblem of the Holly King.

Using sturdy vines like honeysuckle or grape—or whatever is available to you—begin to weave a wreath, wrapping your vines round and round, securing each section with more flexible pieces. Next, create a crescent moon to rest atop the vine, to complete the symbol of the Horned God. It doesn't need to be perfect—in fact, the wilder, the better.

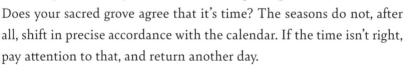

As the Wheel of the Year turns toward the time of the Holly King, it is time to revisit your sacred grove and pay homage to this new energy. With honor and reverence, take down your emblem of the Oak King. Listen to your forest before replacing it. Does your sacred grove agree that it's time? The seasons do not, after all, shift in precise accordance with the calendar. If the time isn't right, pay attention to that, and return another day.

But if it feels to you that, yes, the Holly King has begun his rise, then it is time to hang the emblem you have created in his honor. Find a place for it—it may be that the same location you used for the Oak King is right, or you may require a different spot. Listen to your intuition.

# SUNSET RITUAL

Saying farewell to the day can be a powerful experience. We all have that impulse to take a photograph of a gorgeous sunset, even though we know there will always be another one tomorrow. Consider why that is. Why do we feel the need to hold on to the sunset, to keep it stored forever, either in photograph albums or in our phones? Is there a lingering fear left over from our ancestors' nights spent hiding from the dangers of the dark?

Our nights are safer now, but they are still mysterious. After all, even with the advent of electricity, it is still more difficult to see in the darkness. Sunset is a liminal space—a time between, when it is neither day nor night. All things are possible at sunset.

How will you explore this threshold? Will you light a candle at the moment the sun descends past the horizon to carry its light a little longer? Will you watch for the green flash, the refraction of light moving through the earth's atmosphere? Will you offer thanks to the sun, as well as gratitude to the night?

Whatever you choose to do, take a moment to look within yourself for a threshold you may be standing upon. What is about to shift within you? What do you want to manifest during this time when anything is possible?

# LAMMAS

## *August 1*

Like Imbolc, Lammas is the midpoint between the summer solstice (Litha) and the fall equinox (Mabon). Even though it heralds the arrival of the Holly King, Lammas is often the warmest of the sabbats, as if the Oak King has summoned his forces for one last desperate push.

Despite the heat, Lammas does indeed belong to the Holly King, for it is not a time of sowing but one of reaping. It marks the first harvest of the season, when at last we can secure the benefits of all the work we put in during the time of the Oak King.

Lammas is also known as Lughnasadh, so named for the Celtic warrior sun god Lugh. Although it was named after him, the day actually honors his foster mother, Tailtiu.

Tailtiu was the daughter of Mag Mor, essentially the god of the land. She married Eochaid mac Eirc, the last High King of Ireland, but he was killed by the Tuatha Dé Danann, a term for the fae. The field where he fought lay barren until Tailtiu brought it back to life, strewing it with clover. She remarried a Tuatha Dé Danann and nurtured the young sun god of their people.

When Lugh became king, Tailtiu took it upon herself to rebirth all of Ireland, tilling and clearing the plains to make them arable once more. But she labored too hard and for too long and died providing life for her people. And so, after her death, Lugh made the first day of harvest a celebration of his foster mother by ordering the instigation of the Tailteann Games, demonstrating the health and skill of the Irish in gratitude for her sacrifice.

Tailtiu is the goddess of strength and endurance, which are qualities we will need in the coming seasons. You might consider making a traditional corn dolly in her honor—a small Tailtiu to hang above your door. This doll can be made simply by using a piece of string to craft a head and dress out of a corn husk, or in a more complicated style by weaving dried bits of grain, braiding them, and tying them together, setting your intentions for strength and endurance with each twist.

And then, feast yourself on the fruits of harvest, enjoying fresh, homemade bread and good, hearty beer. Pour a libation onto the earth in thanks for the hard work and sacrifices others have made on our behalf and in recognition for the work we do ourselves, for our own labors and our own strengths.

# PLANTS THAT THRIVE NEAR LAMMAS

## CLOVER
### *Trifolium pratense*

We all know four-leaf clovers are lucky, but even if you don't find one of these genetically mutated versions, tucking a clover into your shoe will bring you good luck. And clover is good for so much more than that—in fact, the druids considered them sacred to the threefold nature of all things, including the earth, the sea, and the sky. They are the sign of good health in body and spirit and promise fidelity to the land and those we love.

### SUGGESTED SPELL

**It is useful to bring clover into any spell, as it boosts the properties of the other ingredients, and it can also be programmed to suit your needs. For a general luck and happiness spell, however, you can press several clovers in a book as on page 36 and scatter them across your threshold, on your windowsills, and above your bed, whispering blessings as you do so.**

## CORN
### *Zea mays*

There are a variety of corn deities, including the Hopi Corn Maidens, the Cherokee goddess Selu, the Aztec goddess Chicomecoatl, and other Indigenous corn mother figures, some of whom literally gave their bodies to feed their children—and us all. For this reason, corn is symbolic of

hazel

honeysuckle

parsley

clover

vervain

corn

holly

fertility as well as safety—it represents the certainty that our basic needs for food, shelter, and companionship will be met. Hanging corn around the home invites her protection.

## SUGGESTED SPELL

**To invite the abundance of corn into your life, use it for manifestation spells. Set aside a few corn husks. Take a piece and tie it into a loop, setting an intention as you do so. Thread a second piece through the first and tie it into another loop, forming the beginnings of a chain. With each link of the chain, add to your intention, making it stronger. Hang your corn chain over your altar.**

# HAZEL
### *Corylus avellana*

Hazelnuts begin to appear on trees near Lammas, as if wisdom is beginning to appear as the year ages. Hazel, or Coll, has strong associations with knowledge and divination. Legend has it that nine hazel trees grew around a sacred spring, and when they dropped their nuts into the water, they were eaten by a salmon—a fish with equally strong powers of wisdom and knowledge, who was later caught by a young boy, who grew up to become the Gaelic hero Fionn mac Cumhaill.

## SUGGESTED SPELL

**Create a divining rod out of hazel by cutting a forked branch—asking permission first, of course. Hold the two prongs beneath your fingers and allow their dips and bends to guide you. Watch how the rod rises and falls—theoretically, a divining rod will rise when it is above an underground spring. But it can also guide you to what you need to**

pay attention to. Perhaps it will guide you to a place where you could sit and meditate. Perhaps it will guide you to a secret, hidden blossom you might otherwise not have noticed. Listen to hazel's wisdom.

# HOLLY
## *Ilex aquifolium*

As the Wheel of the Year turns, holly, or Tinne, becomes prominent, as holly keeps the world alive long after the oak has lost its leaves. Despite its thorny and poisonous nature, there is a sweetness to holly's energy. Hanging holly on a bedpost will invite good dreams as well as good fortune. It also serves as a home for the fairies, and bringing boughs of holly indoors will provide shelter for any otherworldly beings that might venture into your home—and therefore convince them not to harm you while they're there.

## SUGGESTED SPELL

Fill a wide bowl with clean water and arrange a holly sprig within it. Separate a leaf to let it float on its own, then light a very small candle and drip a little wax onto the leaf. Use the hot wax to affix the candle to the leaf. (You'll probably need to extinguish and relight it.) Ask the holly if a decision you've been considering is the right path for you—if the leaf sinks, it probably won't work out well, but if the leaf continues to float and the flame continues to flicker, then holly's powers of good fortune will work on your behalf. If you like, you can put additional sprigs and berries to the water and allow them to soak for a day and a night before draining the basin. You shouldn't drink this holly water, but you can use it to anoint your face, throat, and wrists for protection and good fortune.

# HONEYSUCKLE
## *Lonicera*

Uillean, or honeysuckle, is a climbing vine with sweetly scented, golden flowers. While the plant's berries are mildly poisonous, the nectar is honey-sweet. Sucking the nectar or even rubbing the flowers on the forehead or base of the throat is said to invite love, and sleeping with honeysuckle beneath your pillow can invite prophetic dreams.

### SUGGESTED SPELL

**Sweetening spells are part of a hoodoo tradition meant to encourage others to be kinder to the caster. Honeysuckle clearly lends itself to such spells, but in a slight twist, consider using it to sweeten *yourself* or a relationship that has felt a little sour of late. Collect a good handful of honeysuckle, making sure you get an even number of blossoms, inhaling its sweet fragrance as you go. Let it soothe your soul the way honey soothes the throat. Moving in pairs, suck the nectar from one blossom, then set the next aside for the other person. If you can give these blossoms to this person, do so, but if not, set them in a bowl of water, stirring in a little honey and letting the blossoms float, scenting the air. Their sweetness will travel through the mysterious pathways of water until they reach the other person, whether they know it or not.**

# PARSLEY
## *Petroselinum crispum*

Common parsley, also known as Devil's Oatmeal, was once said to have ventured to the underworld and back nine times before sprouting. Since this plant was thought to have a direct line to death, it was said that if you picked a sprig while speaking an enemy's name, they would die. These days, however, parsley is known more for its protective rather than harmful properties, as if its power has been harnessed and redirected. It also boosts intelligence and creativity, as well as clarity of thought.

## SUGGESTED SPELL

**Parsley lends itself well to kitchen witchery; you can add a sprinkle of it over just about any savory dish you're cooking to offer protection to you and your family. If you'd like to be a bit more deliberate, you can also whisper your intentions as you do so—for example, that everyone has a good day the next day. Parsley is simple but powerful magic.**

# VERVAIN
## *Verbena officinalis*

Also known as the enchanter's herb, vervain is considered both magical and sacred by cultures the world over. The Egyptians believed that vervain sprang from the tears of the goddess Isis when she mourned the death of her brother/husband Osiris, and it was used to treat the wounds of Jesus Christ during the crucifixion. Roman messengers would wear vervain to prove their good intentions and truth, and druids would always harvest vervain in August, near Lammas, and when the Dog Star was visible but neither moon nor sun could be seen in the sky. Despite its renown, vervain is a gentle, soothing herb. It clears the mind and provides a sense of calm and well-being.

## SUGGESTED SPELL

**Whenever you're feeling anxious, turn to vervain. Put a pot of water on to boil and then let it come to rest. Put a teaspoon's worth of dried**

vervain into a tea strainer and pour the water over it. Cover and let it steep for at least ten minutes, surrounded by amethyst, moonstone, and selenite. When it's ready, bring your tea over to your favorite chair and sit comfortably, perhaps covering yourself with a blanket. Before you take your first sip, close your eyes and inhale the steam rising from your cup. Imagine the spirit of the vervain journeying into you through your lungs, clearing away any stress or worry—taking it all away as you exhale. When you swallow your first sip, feel it flowing down your throat and warming you all the way through. Imagine that warmth, that spirit, soaking through your whole body, clearing and soothing as it goes.

# MABON

## *The Fall Equinox*

The odd thing about Mabon is that while we know logically that, like the other sabbats, it has been celebrated for thousands of years, its name is only fifty years old. The 1970s was a time of resurgence for pagan practices, and it was then that Aidan Kelly, a poet and academic, chose the name Mabon for this celebration.

He explained that he wanted to find a European deity that fit the "underworld prisoner" story, as the autumn equinox is the time when Persephone is taken by Hades. The Welsh god Mabon was his inspiration. Mabon was the infant son of the earth goddess Modron, and he was kidnapped and held in the underworld for years, until at last he was rescued by King Arthur and his knights. So we can understand why Kelly chose Mabon; the story certainly does fit that theme.

But the autumn equinox has never really been about honoring the god Mabon; instead, it is the night when the Holly King defeats the Oak King. Mabon is the dark mirror of Imbolc, for while day is equal to night on the fall equinox, just as it is in the spring, we all know it heralds the time when nights will be longer than days.

Mabon is about accepting that truth and finding appreciation and gratitude for it. It's about acknowledging the darkness, both without and within. Half of the year is darker than the other, and half of our lives are spent in darkness, when the sun shines on the other side of the earth. We carry that darkness within as well—not everything is sunshine and light and warmth. We have sadness, and worry, and desires; we have flaws and imperfections.

There is value in all of the above. Our darkness can be the source of our creativity, our dreams, and our passions. It is something to be celebrated.

On Mabon, we honor the darkness. We welcome its sheltering protection and its mysterious and mystical powers. On the night of the autumn equinox, visit your sacred grove. If it's safe and permissible, light a small bonfire there—if not, simply use a lantern. Sit within that pool of light, which makes the darkness around you seem even deeper. Close your eyes and watch the light flicker against your lids. Then listen to the sounds of the night. Hear the trees rustle. Many of the animals have gone to rest, but you'll still sense some birds or bats or insects. Listen to the darkness without, and then listen for the darkness within you. What do you dream of? What do you wish for?

If you like, you can write down a series of intentions for this darker season and cast them into the fire—or you can keep them close, tucked beneath a pillow when you sleep.

## PLANTS THAT THRIVE NEAR MABON

# BLACKTHORN

### *Prunus spinosa*

Straith, the blackthorn, is a very masculine tree, with properties of control and strength. As such, it is also a tree of protection, with dense and thorny branches. Staffs or walking sticks made of blackthorn can withstand treks across the length of Scotland and will support you as you hike the wildernesses of your home. And yet, for all that, its fruit is edible and nourishing—sloe, or blackthorn berry, is best known for flavoring gin, as it is quite sour.

### SUGGESTED SPELL

**Harvesting sloe berries is a tricky process, as the tree will fight you with its thorns even after having granted its permission, as if you must still endure its trials. But keep at it—blackthorn may be fierce, but by proving yourself worthy, you will gain its everlasting strength. Pick your sloes after the first frost, as the fruit will be sweeter, and gather about**

grape

ivy

blackthorn

mandrake

daisy

goldenrod

pomegranate

seven cups' worth. Add them to a large saucepan and cover them with a quart of water and the juice of one lemon. Bring the mixture to a boil and simmer it for fifteen minutes, stirring frequently and smashing the berries against the pan with the back of a wooden spoon. Turn off the heat, and strain out the liquid—you can reserve the cooked berries to make a compote or chutney if you like. Return the liquid to the pan and stir in two to three cups of sugar, depending on how sweet you want your syrup to be. Simmer for another ten minutes, then allow it to cool. You can add this syrup to sparkling water or serve it over ice cream, turning to blackthorn whenever you need a little structure in your life.

# DAISY
## *Bellis perennis*

It is said that the daisy got its name from the phrase "day's eye," because it will open its petals every morning to gaze at the sun and close them again at night. While daisy is often thought of as a spring flower, it blooms all the way into the deep fall. Daisy's whimsy and childlike spirit always brings optimism and even joy on the darkest of days. Daisies are ideal for dream magic, and you can keep a bouquet of daisies next to your bed or place a single blossom beneath your pillow to invite good dreams.

### SUGGESTED SPELL

Consider the old game in which you pluck a daisy petal by petal to see if someone "loves me or loves me not." Now we can change that game from a divination spell to a spell for internal knowledge. When you are facing a difficult decision and don't know what you truly want, pluck a daisy. Assign one path to the first petal, and the second path to the next, alternating as you go. When you reach the last petal, check in with yourself.

**Are you disappointed by the daisy's answer, or are you relieved? Either way, you now have information about which path is right for** *you.*

# GOLDENROD
## *Solidago*

Goldenrod is primarily used for luck and prosperity magic. You can carry a sprig of goldenrod with you to an important event where you need to perform at your best or use it in a spell bag, nestled with clover, citrine, and aventurine. It is connected to sun magic, bringing energy and warmth and power into your home, and can be used to boost healing.

### SUGGESTED SPELL

**Goldenrod can also be a useful divining rod, much like the hazel divining rod on page 60. Cut a sprig of goldenrod near the base—always asking permission first—and use it to guide you, following its nodding head as you walk. It might bring you to an item you've lost or lead you to a place where you can rest and meditate, recharging your own energy.**

# GRAPE
## *Vitis vinifera*

Mabon is the time of the vine or Muin—the protective climber who also invites creativity. Grapevines are particularly passionate and speak to the wildness of our emotions as well as the deep truths of our hearts. Eating grapes with thought and care, being mindful of their taste—even peeling them first to prolong the experience—can help you pause and take the time to understand your own feelings.

## SUGGESTED SPELL

Brew a batch of mulled wine by heating up a bottle of dry red wine until it is just steaming. Add a cinnamon stick, a cup of apple cider, the peel of one orange, and three cloves. Let it steep over low heat for at least thirty minutes, but don't allow it to come to a boil. Serve hot and enjoy it with friends on a chilly autumn evening—it will help you understand each other's emotions.

# IVY

### *Hedera helix*

As is proclaimed in the old winter song, the ivy is the partner to the holly, and when they are both "full grown"—i.e., when the year draws to a close—their powers of protection are at their greatest. Ivy, or Got, is also useful for binding magic, but rather than seeking to bind someone else, consider using ivy to mend a relationship or seal your own energies from outside forces.

## SUGGESTED SPELL

Because ivy is so flexible and abundant, it is ideal for simple weaving. You can either wind a strand of ivy into a humble crown that you can wear while performing a ritual or use several strands to create a sacred circle that you can sit within. Ivy will encircle you, creating a powerful force field that will protect you while also improving the efficacy of your spells.

# MANDRAKE
## *Mandragora*

While wild mandrake does not grow plentifully in the United States, it is simple enough to cultivate. And while, with alternate names like Herb of Circe, Sorcerer's Root, and Witch's Mannikin, it has a reputation for being an "evil" plant, there is no such thing. Just as magic is simply a force, plants, poisonous or otherwise, are simply themselves. Like many of the plants that thrive near Mabon, mandrake is ideal for both creativity and protection magic, and it can increase the potency of any spell.

### SUGGESTED SPELL

**Legends say that mandrakes are actually small creatures, and it can be fun to work with them as if this is, in fact, the case. After asking permission, carefully pull up the mandrake as you would a carrot, dislodging it from the earth. Bring it inside and cut off the leaves, then scrub it clean under running water. When it dries, give it a place on your altar for a time, leaving it simple offerings of coins or found objects. It will work its magic for you.**

# POMEGRANATE
## *Punica granatum*

The rules of Hades's Underworld were remarkably similar to the rules of the fae: as long as you consumed neither food nor drink, they could not keep you. And so, when Zeus demanded that Hades release Persephone, Hades had no choice, because Persephone had eaten nothing during her time with him. But, pleading with her to stay, he made one final attempt and offered her a pomegranate. Persephone, knowing all too well what she did, chose in the end to consume six tiny pomegranate seeds, making it so that she would remain queen of the Underworld for six months out of the year. Because of this tale, this mysterious, vibrantly colored fruit is best known for its love magic, but it is also useful for prosperity, divination, and creativity spells.

## SUGGESTED SPELL

Take inspiration from Persephone and set aside six pomegranate seeds to eat with intention. Perhaps you can use this as an opportunity to seal a decision that you have been struggling with. Use by either popping them in a blender and gently pulsing until the juice separates but the inner seeds remain intact, or by breaking them down with a mortar and pestle. Strain out the juice—reserving some to drink, of course!—and dip a fine-tipped brush into it. Using the pomegranate juice as ink, write down an intention, spell, or sigil onto a piece of paper. After that, you can either store the paper beneath your pillow, tuck it on your altar or into a spell bag, or burn it to release it.

# TWILIGHT RITUAL

The gloaming, that shift from dusk to twilight, can be the most mysterious time of them all. It is that moment when we can still see, but not as
well—when outlines are fuzzy and our depth perception is not quite as

reliable. Your creative mind has to fill in the spaces between, like an artist reconstructing a faded painting.

If it's safe to do so, take a walk in the dark of twilight, without a flashlight or any other sources of light. Your eyes will struggle, focusing on this shape and that, sometimes misinterpreting what you see, so that a branch will appear to be a looming figure or a fern will seem like a small creature. Ask yourself which version of what you see is true. Yes, logically we know the fern is not a creature . . . but what if, in the twilight, you possess a different kind of vision? Perhaps this is what is meant by "seeing fairies."

As you wander and allow your eyes to interpret things as they choose to, let that sense of wonder and imagination seep into your soul. All things are possible now, when the world is malleable. And remember—this time of promise and potential comes *every single day*. It is always available to you. That sense of wonder, that chance of seeing fairies, is something you can carry with you all day and every day. How will you choose to see the world?

# SAMHAIN

## *October 31*

On this night, the Crone aspect of the Threefold Goddess—also known as the Cailleach—rides the wind, stripping the leaves from the trees as the year decays. What do you want her to take with her? What do you no longer need to carry?

As Halloween, or All Hallow's Eve, was derived from Samhain, it's easy to think of them as being synonymous. After all, there are a lot of commonalities—dressing up in costumes, bobbing for apples, and a general spooky vibe is a pretty accurate way of describing them both. And, like all the sabbats, Samhain is at heart a celebration of life.

But it is also a celebration of death, in a way that modern-day Halloween doesn't really get into. We all know that death is an unavoidable fact of life, but we tend not to acknowledge it unless we are absolutely forced to. That makes sense—who wants to live beneath the shadow of death? But just as we acknowledge and celebrate the darkness on Mabon, on Samhain we acknowledge the presence of death with honor and respect.

It is said that on Samhain the veil between worlds is thin and the dead walk among us. Sometimes that might mean actual ghosts and the sensation of another presence in a room that you cannot explain. But it can also mean thinking of memories of loved ones who have passed—those who are gone but always with us.

Ancestral magic is particularly powerful on Samhain. If you are seeking the advice of those who came before you, or simply want to feel their love and support, consider putting together an ancestral altar. You can dedicate it to specific members of your family or reach back past the time of your own memory to those who came even earlier—whose names you may not even know—but who have an influence over you nevertheless. You can gather photographs, heirlooms, or other mementos of your ancestors and group them together, lighting a candle for each family member represented. Ask for their wisdom and offer gratitude for their support.

If you want, you can take this even further and put together a traditional Samhain feast of the dead, also known as a dumb supper. Set an extra place at the head of your table, where the ancestors will sit. Serve them food and drink as you serve yourself, but remain silent and never look at their chair directly, keeping your head bowed in respect. When you've finished eating, take the extra plate outside as an offering to the fairies.

The fairies, after all, are said to ride on this night, and legend has it that if you've lost a loved one to the fae, this is your chance to win them back—as in the story of Tam Lin when Janet, pregnant with his child, held on to him no matter what, even as he shifted from one monstrous form to the next, until the Queen of the Fairies had no choice but to release him.

What does that mean, from a modern perspective? The answer is, as always—whatever we want it to. Perhaps you might consider something you've lost, whether it's a passion, a desired outcome, or a friend. In this case, the loss doesn't mean death, but something that feels out of your grasp. Let the energy of Samhain—and the stubborn love of Janet—inspire you to reach for it again.

## PLANTS THAT THRIVE NEAR SAMHAIN

# APPLE
### *Malus domestica*

Quert, or the apple, is somehow simultaneously wholesome and representative of the forbidden—of knowledge and passion. That knowledge can include the unknown, as apples are also used for prophesying. But their wholesome aspects can be found in their powers of healing, and if you cut an apple into three pieces and bury them beneath a waning moon, you can invite good health into your home. Burying apples is also a way to feed any wandering spirits that may feel lost and alone.

## SUGGESTED SPELL

**Apple divination is best used for simple yes/no questions. Take an apple and cut it in half, separating the top and bottom. Open it up and peer at the shape of a flower formed by the seed cluster. How many dark seeds can you see? Typically, an odd number indicates a no and an even number indicates a yes to your question, but listen to your intuition.**

# MARIGOLD
## *Calendula officinalis*

Marigolds are used to communicate with the dead, and they serve as an offering and a guide. Like sunflowers, marigolds turn their heads to follow the sun, and it feels as though their bright crowns light a path for our ancestors to follow. They are also particularly useful for dream magic, helping to boost intuition and psychic abilities and providing a gentle, soothing rest.

## SUGGESTED SPELL

**Just before going to sleep, prepare a marigold spell bath. You can use fresh or dried flowers or a combination of the two. Heat the bath as hot as you can make it while still remaining comfortable, then scatter in your blossoms, breaking up the petals. Light a few candles and close your eyes, allowing your body to relax and be permeated by the energy of the blossoms. When you're ready, climb out, but don't rinse off. Pat yourself dry, then get into bed. Inhale the herbal, verdant scent of the**

marigolds on your skin, and ask them to invite your ancestors into your dreams.

# MUGWORT
## *Artemisia vulgaris*

Mugwort is an extremely powerful plant and should be used with intention and care. It is protective—as so many plants are—but it is best known for its psychic powers; it can provide prophetic dreams and even assist with astral projection or producing visions. It doesn't contain any psychoactive properties (i.e., it's not a hallucinogen). It simply helps open your third eye—that place just above and between your brows, also known as the chakra *ajna*.

## SUGGESTED SPELL

The most effective way to work with mugwort is by brewing a tincture; just a small amount is extremely potent. If you have access to fresh mugwort, collect it on the night of a full moon and hang it upside down to dry. If not, you can purchase dried mugwort online or in some health food stores. Add a quarter cup of dried mugwort to a jar and cover it with vodka. Let it steep for a full lunar cycle, surrounded by lapis lazuli to help boost its psychic powers. When it's ready, strain out the liquid and take a teaspoonful before sleep or meditation or whenever you want your intuition to be at its most powerful.

*rosemary*

*apple*

*marigold*

*mugwort*

*reed*

*pumpkin*

*spindle*

# PUMPKIN
## *Cucurbita pepo*

October wouldn't be October without pumpkins, and carving a jack-o'-lantern is a ritual protective spell that dates back to the 1800s. Before that, British and Irish immigrants to the United States would use turnips for the same purpose, but with pumpkins so readily available in North America, not to mention larger, the tradition shifted. Jack-o'-lanterns are named for Stingy Jack, a man who made a deal with the devil and won, and so did not lose his soul—but was also not welcome in heaven. So he was doomed to wander the earth, and the pumpkins (or turnips) were carved and lit to warn him away. In addition to protective magic, pumpkins are also good for prosperity spells.

### SUGGESTED SPELL

After you've carved your pumpkin, save the stem and the seeds. Allow the stem to dry completely, then add it to your altar during the time of the sabbat to bring power to any manifestation spells you may wish to cast. Roast the seeds in the oven and save some for a prosperity spell jar, consuming the rest. Create your manifestation spell jar by layering your ingredients into a small glass jar, sealing it, and anointing it with candle wax. What should you include? You may want to consider adding some aventurine, jade, or citrine, as well as mint, clover, winter aconite, and basil.

# REED
## *Phragmites australis*

The term *reed* refers to a wide variety of aquatic grasses, but phragmites are the most widespread. You can see their great heads nodding alongside highways and in fields and marshes where they shelter and hide wildlife. In truth, they can easily take over an ecosystem, but when managed, they are wonderfully useful. The entire plant is edible, and the stems make delightful drinking straws. Reeds, or nGeatal, have been used for millennia to weave baskets, purify water, thatch roofs, and best of all, to make music. They are still used for this purpose today in oboes, clarinets, and other wind instruments. Reeds are best in protection magic, as well as in summoning.

### SUGGESTED SPELL

**Cut a single phragmites near its base, then trim it until you have a hollow straw. Before putting it to your lips, consider what you want to call forth. What parts of your identity do you want to summon? What facets of yourself or others do you want to embody? As you blow on your pipe, don't worry about making a sound—it's about what your breath puts into the air around you. Use it to summon that which you need most.**

# ROSEMARY
## *Rosmarinus officinalis*

Rosemary is for remembrance, which makes it particularly appropriate for Samhain, when we strive to honor those who have come before us. It is a wise and protective plant, seeking to create connection through memory; it can help maintain love in relationships, boost recall when you are struggling to remember everything on your to-do list, and keep you safe while traveling, as you remember that home is always there for you.

## SUGGESTED SPELL

**Like thyme, sage, and other culinary magical herbs, rosemary is very useful for kitchen witchery, and you can simply add it as an ingredient whenever you feel you need its support. But because rosemary is so fragrant, it's also quite useful for scent magic. Collect a handful of fresh rosemary—a half cup's worth will do—and chop it roughly to release the juices. Cover the rosemary with sweet almond or another neutral oil, and let this herbal oil steep for at least two weeks. When you're ready, strain out the plant matter and use the oil either directly on your skin or melt some beeswax and mix it in to make a balm you can rub on your temples, over your heart, and on the soles of your feet. As you do so, call on rosemary to help you remember what's most important to you.**

# SPINDLE
### *Euonymus*

The spindle tree is also known as Our or burning bush, for its fiery red fruits and leaves. Its wood is so hard it can be carved sharply, so it was used to make—you guessed it—spindles for spinning wool. Its usefulness is tied to its properties of hard work—but this is the type of hard work that we do *for* something—a labor of love. In fact, spindle is also tied in with the concept of family, the responsibilities we share, and the love we hold for the people closest to us.

## SUGGESTED SPELL

When we think of long-ago spindles, a single tale comes to mind—
Sleeping Beauty. The spindle took her out of her own story, and for a
hundred years she was away from her labors and her family. With that
in mind, take a sharp twig of spindle and gently press it against the tip
of your finger. (There's no need to draw blood!) But here, rather than
exiting from the commitments and responsibilities of your life, let the
spindle remind you of what it's all *for.* Remember why and for whom you
do what you do, and give yourself a gentle prick for every person, every
reason, behind your labors of love.

# YULE

## *The Winter Solstice*

For one instant on the winter solstice, the sun stands still in the sky, frozen at the peak of the Holly King's powers. And then the earth's tilt begins to reverse, angling so that his hold over us begins to wane.

But this night is the longest night, and on Yule, we honor the darkness, even as we celebrate the beginning of the return of the light. The aspect of the Holly King known as the Horned God rides on this night, leading the Wild Hunt across the land—and perhaps the sky—sweeping the earth with untamed abandon.

If this feels a bit fearsome, that's only sensible—the structure and predictability of the Oak King is nowhere to be found on this night. But it is also inspiring, and the thrill of *possibility,* of there being no rules and only potential, can lead us to stretch ourselves, as we explore ways of being we had never considered. And yet, for all that, the Holly King's namesake is a protective plant, providing shelter and safety beneath its thorny hedges all year long.

Celebrations of Yule typically include feasting and carousing because, well, that's just how sabbats are! You could invite those closest to you for a feast and light a bonfire with a traditional Yule log. Long ago, Yule logs were essentially giant tree limbs that were hauled into the hearth and slid into its gaping maw, burning away over the course of the twelve nights after Yule—or after Christmas, once pagan and Christian beliefs intermingled. Most of us don't have fireplaces the size of tree trunks these days, but if you set aside a certain log, you can designate it as your Yule log, even if it isn't large enough to last the full twelve nights. Sprinkle it with libations of mulled wine, mead, salt, or flour, setting your intentions for the coming days of light. When the log has just about burned down completely, carefully fish it out of the fire and let it cool, saving this piece to kindle your fire for your next Yule celebration.

Alternatively, you can visit your sacred grove for a more private ritual to honor the longest night. Bring a candle with you, ideally one in a jar or other container so that it is protected from the wind and the melting wax won't burn your fingertips. Just at the moment of the solstice, right when the sun goes down, light your candle. Raise it to the west, honoring the setting sun. Turn, and raise it to the east, saluting the dawn's coming light. Raise it to the south, where, on the other side of the planet, others are celebrating the longest day. And finally, raise your candle to the cold, dark north—the land of the Holly King—in gratitude for his mystery and protection.

Take a moment to set an intention, either by thought or spoken aloud. You might even sing in chorus with the trees that surround you. Take comfort in the darkness, within the circle of light that you have created, and know that from this moment on, everything will be brighter.

## PLANTS THAT THRIVE NEAR YULE

# ELDER
### *Sambucus*

Ruis, or elder, is alternatively known as elderberry, a fast-growing hedge-like plant that hosts a variety of moths and butterflies in the warmer months. It can grow under just about any conditions, but despite this hardiness, it is also quite brittle, bending and breaking easily. This duality is reflected in its magical powers, as it is both an invitation to the riskier, more mysterious aspects of life—as represented by fairies—and a force for protection from those same aspects. Burning elder indoors could invite demons, but traditionally branches of elder were buried with the dead to protect them from the same.

## SUGGESTED SPELL

Working with this duality comes down to intention—do you want to call on elder's powers of protection or of wildness? Crafting an amulet out of elder while setting those intentions will align its powers in the direction you're looking for. After asking permission, cut a small piece of elder wood. If you're hoping for protection, cut it in the light, but if you want mystery, cut it in shadow. Take a piece of string and wrap it round the twig—tie one knot above, and one knot below. For protection, let your amulet rest in the sunlight for one day, surrounded by peridot and pyrite, and for mystery, let your amulet rest in the moonlight for one night, surrounded by mookaite and chrysocolla.

# JUNIPER
## *Juniperus*

Juniper is connected with both protection and creativity and was sacred to the Syrian fertility goddess Astarte. It is also said that a juniper sheltered Jesus as an infant when he hid from King Herod's soldiers. Juniper's dusky, dark blue "berries" are actually tiny, fleshy pine cones and can be crushed and pressed for their juices, which have a spicy bitter flavor—in fact, juniper is best known for its use in flavoring gin.

## SUGGESTED SPELL

The best way to invite creativity is to start creating! For juniper, you might consider creating your own batch of gin. Gin is essentially just flavored vodka, but it is a very specific flavor. Distilleries will use extractions and whatnot, but to craft your own gin you can simply make "compound gin"—what used to be known as "bathtub gin." For a 750 ml bottle of vodka, you'll need at least two tablespoons of fresh or dried juniper berries. You may want to include additional botanicals, including other herbs for creativity, like mugwort and orange peel. Put all of your botanicals to a large clean jar and cover with the vodka, then allow your gin to steep for a full day and night. Taste and continue to steep if necessary, checking every day. (You don't want to overflavor and create a tincture instead!) Strain your potion when it tastes right to you, and then enjoy whenever you need a boost of creativity.

# MISTLETOE
## *Viscum album*

Mistletoe is believed to be one of the most magical plants known today. Despite its reputation as a love charm—though it is that—it has also been a bringer of peace. In olden days if enemies met in the forest and found themselves beneath mistletoe, they were obliged to lay down arms and seek a peaceful solution. Because of this tradition, mistletoe would be brought indoors in Nordic countries for Yuletide feasting so that any disputes between clans would have to be set aside for the festivities.

### SUGGESTED SPELL
Despite its magical nature, mistletoe is actually a parasite—it climbs the oak tree and eats away at it in a natural depiction of the battle between the Oak King and the Holly King. Historically, druidic elders would ritually harvest the mistletoe from the oaks in the days after Yule—but they would wear holly to avoid offending the Holly King, as it was still the time of his rule. If you notice any mistletoe growing nearby, on oaks or other trees, you may want to don some holly and pull the mistletoe down. But bring it home with you and hang it from your ceiling, to invite peace, good luck, and love into your home.

mistletoe

yew

witch hazel

myrtle

juniper

elder

pine

# MYRTLE
## *Myrtus communis*

Myrtle acts as a preservative force, much in the way ice and cold can preserve our food. It helps love sustain tribulation, which is why it is often found in bridal bouquets—and perhaps why it was also sacred to Aphrodite. It also preserves youthfulness, and planting myrtle along each side of the doorway to your home will invite peace, love, and prosperity. It is said, in fact, that myrtle was the scent most prominent in the Garden of Eden—that most peaceful, loving, and eternal place.

### SUGGESTED SPELL

Use the aromatic myrtle to craft a perfume oil—myrtle is a prominent note in a variety of luxury perfumes. Either add a few drops of myrtle essential oil to a neutral carrier oil like jojoba or sweet almond oil, or if the fresh plant is available to you, add the flowers, berries, leaves, and small bits of the wood to a mortar and pestle, bruising and melding them. Place this mixture in a jar and cover with your carrier oil, allowing the crushed myrtle to steep in sunlight for at least two weeks before use. Anoint yourself with myrtle oil as Aphrodite would, whenever you seek love and/or youthfulness, and whenever you want to feel your own sense of love and peace—as myrtle will call forth the calm and self-love we all carry within.

# PINE

## *Pinus*

The strength of Ifin, or pine, is not just in its longevity and evergreen nature, but also in its protective and peaceful properties. At the same time, it is also known for its courage and endurance, as it withstands the long cold. The Iroquois believe that the white pine is the "tree of peace," and in Japan, pine is hung over the entrance of the home to invite joy. Pine needles can be burned to remove negative energy, and pine cones can be burned to invite health and creativity.

### SUGGESTED SPELL

Because of pine's varied magical properties, it's best to work with it as a whole, and in all areas of life. Whenever you feel your home is in need of a good energetic and physical cleansing, turn to pine. Begin by taking a pine branch and using it to sweep your floors and windowsills, collecting all the stagnant energy or negativity that may have gathered there. (You can follow up with a regular broom afterward.) Next, add some pine needles to a pot of water and set it on the stove to boil, releasing the scent of the pine into the air. Let this simmer for at least an hour, then strain—you can use this pine water as a floor wash. Finally, collect all that you have gathered over recent months that you no longer need— receipts, bills that have been paid, old reminder notes—and if it's safe to do so, add them to a fire. Throw in any remaining pine needles, including from your pine broom. Toss in a few pine cones, and with each cone that you burn, set an intention for what you are asking it to release from you, as you make space for joy and love instead.

# WITCH HAZEL
## *Hamamelis*

Amhancholl, or witch hazel, is a cleansing herb of new beginnings. It can help to heal a wounded heart and can aid in divining where your path will lead when it feels like you've reached a dead end. It is often found in skin care products as it is a powerful astringent, and witch hazel is still used today as divining rods to determine where a well should be dug.

### SUGGESTED SPELL

**Turn to witch hazel when you feel like your spirits are lowest and the world is at its darkest. Even if it feels difficult to get out of bed, go for a walk and collect some witch hazel. This is a tree that longs to be of service, so in this case, if you aren't up for a full ritual, you can simply ask permission in your heart as you take a small sprig. Put it in the pocket of your coat or tuck it into your bag, but be sure to carry it with you for a little while, even after any leaves or flowers have wilted—your spirits will lift.**

# YEW
## *Taxus*

Yew, or Iodhadh, has been called the tree of the dead, and legend has it that yew wands could be used by necromancers to raise corpses for undead servants . . . but it is perhaps better understood as the tree of the crossroads. Yew trees are often found in graveyards—in fact, somewhere around five hundred English churches were built alongside yew trees, with the yews being older than the buildings. Perhaps they were meant to encourage the spirits of the dead to stay at rest? Or perhaps they allow clearer communication with our ancestors? Either way, this powerful plant is highly poisonous (hence its inclusion by the three weird sisters in their potion in *Macbeth*), but also highly flexible, and longbows such as those used by Robin Hood were made of yew. If this makes it seem like yews have been around for a while—they have! In the center of Scotland grows the Fortingall Yew, which is purported to be anything from two thousand to nine thousand years old. Similarly, Mayo in Ireland is the largest yew forest in the world, and there are indications that it has been there since the last ice age. Yew lives just about forever and reproduces by rooting drooping branches of older trees, which spring up anew in a natural example of the cycle of life—and the Wheel of the Year.

## SUGGESTED SPELL

**Craft a yew wand by taking a twig from a yew tree—as always, ask permission! Using a small knife, scrape away the bark, cleaning off any knobs or smaller branches. Leave one of the ends jagged. Find a bare patch of earth, and use your yew wand to draw a sigil. Maybe you'd like to use Ogham, or perhaps the Norse runic system. Choose your spell wisely, as yew spells are not only strong, but everlasting.**

# MIDNIGHT RITUAL

Historically, witches would fly at midnight. We can all conjure up images of black-gowned women seated upon a broom, soaring across a cloudless night sky. But the consensus is that, like fairies, that's probably an allegory, and any "flying" that actually took place occurred only in the mind.

The "flying ointment" that witches would apply in order to take to the air is typically described as including:

- **Belladonna**
- **Fly agaric**
- **Foxglove**
- **Hellebore**
- **Hemlock**

- **Henbane**
- **Mandrake root**
- **Monkshood**
- **Poppy**
- **Wolfsbane**

Historical accounts—as given by Christian men, including Francis Bacon, chancellor under Queen Elizabeth—state that witches would include the "fat of children dinged out of their graves" as well as bat blood and vulture fat. These ingredients are, to put it mildly, extremely unlikely, and their inclusion in these descriptions are likely the result of fear and misogyny.

Vulture fat aside, you may have noticed a few commonalities in the other listed ingredients—they are often hallucinogenic. There are certainly plenty of Indigenous traditions around the consumption of entheogens—naturally occurring psychoactives—for spiritual and cultural ceremonial use, and it stands to reason that this could have occurred in long-ago witchy communities as well. It is certainly easy enough to imagine the forest witches of yore walking with bare feet among the moss and roots, holding secret rituals that honor nature in all her feminine power.

That said, it's not a great idea to follow these recipes and craft your own flying ointment to see where it takes you—these substances are all classified as poisonous and can be very harmful or even deadly.

Instead, consider a different recipe. Crafting a nonlethal and non-entheogenic—but still magical!—flying ointment is a way to honor and participate in those traditions while still remaining safe. To brew your own flying ointment, gather together the following herbs:

1 tablespoon juniper, fresh
or dried

¼ teaspoon dried rosemary or
1 tablespoon fresh

¼ teaspoon dried mugwort or
1 tablespoon fresh

¼ teaspoon dried mint or
1 tablespoon fresh

¼ teaspoon dried yarrow or
1 tablespoon fresh

¼ teaspoon dried lavender or
1 tablespoon fresh

¼ teaspoon dried sage or
1 tablespoon fresh

Combine all the ingredients in a mortar and pestle and crush them together, releasing their scents and melding them. Add them to a glass jar and cover with a half cup of carrier oil. Let the jar sit where the sun and moon will shine upon it for a full lunar cycle, surrounded by amethyst, calcite, chrysocolla, hematite, lapis lazuli, mookaite, or opal.

At the end of the lunar cycle, strain your herbal oil out into a saucepan. Put the heat on low, and stir in half an ounce to an ounce of beeswax. (The more beeswax you use, the firmer your ointment will be.) When the beeswax has melted, remove the pan from the heat and pour the ointment into a wide-mouthed jar. Let it cool completely before use.

When you're ready to fly, visit your sacred grove. Find a place where you can sit nestled beneath the branches. Take just a bit of your flying ointment and anoint your third eye. If you like, you can anoint each of your chakras, as well as your wrists and the soles of your feet. Inhale the scent of the herbs, and let their magic fill you. Where do you want to fly? What do you want to experience? Let your imagination take hold—for it, too, is magic—and allow your mind to wander as it wills, listening to the silence of the forest at night—a silence that isn't quite silence, but is filled with mystery and possibility.

# REWILDING

Embracing the life of a forest witch is both an honor and a responsibility. Every offering we make to the forest is meaningful, whether it's a libation, a whisper of thanks, a clearing out of invasives, or even a donation to help preserve larger sacred groves like the Amazon Rainforest.

We receive so much from the forest—and by extension, from all of nature—whether in the form of sustenance, shelter, protection, inspiration, love, beauty, divination, wisdom, healing . . . the list goes on and on. But more than that, we receive *ourselves*.

Albert Einstein said, "Look deep into nature, and then you will understand everything better." And John Muir said, "Into the forest I go to lose my mind and find my soul." These complementary observations are both true—we gain an intellectual and scientific understanding of the world from forests, as well as the practical realities of food and shelter. But we also gain something deeper—the version of ourselves that exists beneath the anxieties, the everyday tasks, and the racing thoughts that occupy our restless nights. We are more than the everyday—we are as eternal as the forest, and also as alive. We carry the wisdom of the forest, as well as its magic.

In your journey of rewilding, never forget that you are wild already, for the forest is within you, even as you bathe in its arms.

# ACKNOWLEDGMENTS

This book was a gift.

I am so lucky to work with such amazing people, at such an amazing publisher. I never, ever take it for granted, and I value everything they do. Shannon Fabricant, Kristin Kiser, Susan Van Horn, Amber Morris, Ashley Benning, Amy Cianfrone, Kara Thornton, Ana-Maria Bonner, Elizabeth Parks, Annie Brag, Betsey Hulsebosch, and everyone else in the Running Press family, I honestly cannot tell you how much I appreciate your hard work and your creativity, as well as the sense of joy and magic you all bring.

For Dave, Neil, and Annie—thanks for walking the forests with me.

# INDEX

cherry tree, 22–23
chrysocolla, xx
cities, x
clootie wells, 8–9
clover, 58
compound gin, 89–90
corn, 58–60
crocus, 11–12
Crone, 76
crystals
  magical gifts, xix
  primer on, xx–xxi
cyclamen, 23–24

**D**
daffodil, 24–25
daisy, 69–70
dawn ritual, 5–6
dead, tree of the, 95
death, celebration of, 77–78
Demeter, xxxi, 26
disgorging head, 3
divining rods, 60–61, 70, 94
dumb supper, 77

**E**
eggs
  blown, 18–19
  hanging, with intention, 18
  naturally dyed, 19
Einstein, Albert, 101
elder tree
  in Ogham alphabet, xxv
  personality, xxx
  suggested spell, 89
  symbolism, 88

elm tree
  in Ogham alphabet, xxvi
  suggested spell, 12
  symbolism, 12
entheogens, 97
Eostre (goddess), 18

**F**
fairies
  attraction to primrose, 35
  attraction to roses, 46
  attraction to thyme, 47
  on October 31, 78
  providing shelter for, 61
  at twilight, 75
  valuing and fearing, 35–36
  warding off, 30
  what they mean to you, 48
fall equinox, 65–66
feast of the dead, 77–78
fern, 41–42
flower viewing, 23
fluorite, xx
flying ointment, 13, 96–98
foliate head, 3
Fortingall Yew, 95

**G**
ghosts, 77
gin, 89–90
gloaming, 74
goldenrod, 70
gorse
  in Ogham alphabet, xxvi
  suggested spell, 25
  symbolism, 25

grapes, 70–71
Graves, Robert, xxiii
graveyards, 95
Green Man, 2–4
grove, in Ogham alphabet, xxvi

**H**
Hades, xxxii, 26, 66, 72
Halloween, 77
*hanami* (flower viewing), 23
hawthorn tree
   in Ogham alphabet, xxv
   personality, xxviii
   suggested spell, 35
   symbolism, 35
hazel tree
   in Ogham alphabet, xxv
   personality, xxix
   suggested spell, 60–61
   symbolism, 60
heather
   in Ogham alphabet, xxvi
   suggested spell, 43
   symbolism, 42
hellebore, 13–14
herbs. *See also specific herbs*
   harvesting, xviii
   pruning and thinning, xviii
Holly King
   battles with Oak King, 17–18
   emblem (Horned God), 52–53
   at fall equinox, 66
   what he represents, xxxiii
holly tree
   in Ogham alphabet, xxv
   personality, xxix

suggested spell, 61
symbolism, 61
honey, 40
honeysuckle
   in Ogham alphabet, xxvi
   suggested spell, 62
   symbolism, 62
Horned God, 52–53, 87

**I**
Imbolc, 7–16
Isis (goddess), 63
ivy
   in Ogham alphabet, xxv
   personality, xxx
   suggested spell, 71
   symbolism, 71

**J**
jade, xx
Jesus, 89
juniper, 89–90

**K**
Kelly, Aidan, 66

**L**
Lammas, 56–64
lapis lazuli, xx
lavender, 43–45
liminal space, 14
Litha, 39–48
livestock, 8
Lughnasadh, 57